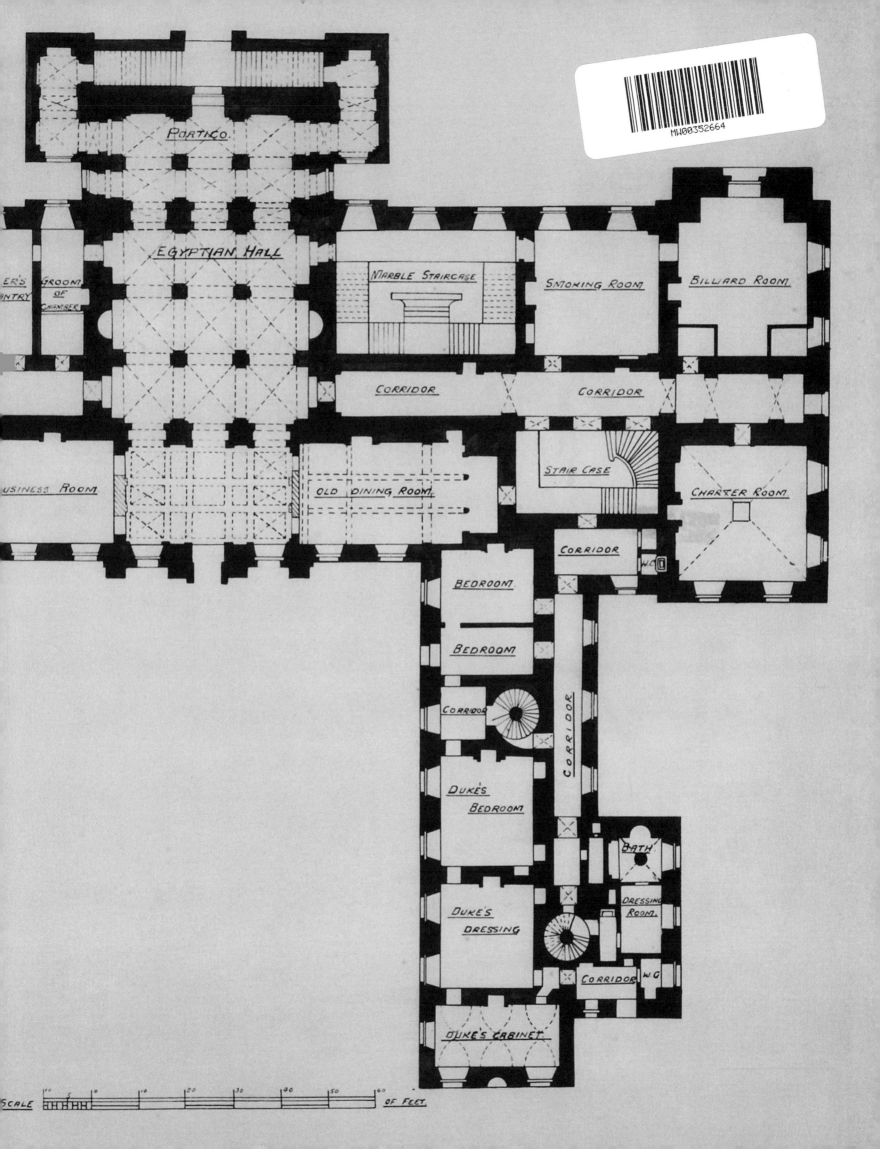

PORTICO.

EGYPTIAN HALL

MARBLE STAIRCASE

SMOKING ROOM

BILLIARD ROOM

GROOM OF CHAMBER

ER'S ANTRY

CORRIDOR

CORRIDOR

STAIR CASE

BUSINESS ROOM.

OLD DINING ROOM.

CHARTER ROOM.

CORRIDOR

W.C.

BEDROOM.

BEDROOM.

CORRIDOR

CORRIDOR

DUKE'S BEDROOM

BATH

DRESSING ROOM.

DUKE'S DRESSING

CORRIDOR
W.C.

DUKE'S CABINET

SCALE ⊢⊢⊢⊢⊢⊢ 10 20 30 40 50 60 OF FEET.

SCOTLAND'S
LOST HOUSES

February 15, 2008

Dear Bob,

Happy 70th Birthday!

We love you very much.

all our love,

David & Mary

xo

The National Trust
for Scotland

SCOTLAND'S
LOST HOUSES

Ian Gow

Aurum

For Jane Thomas

ACKNOWLEDGEMENTS

I am extremely grateful to Graham Coster at Aurum for asking me to undertake this book but embarrassed at the length of time it finally took. My first debt is to the late Giles Worsley, who gave sound advice for following in his footsteps. It is always a pleasure to have an excuse to work in the congenial Photographic Library at *Country Life* under the inspired direction of Camilla Costello and her team. At *Country Life* too both Jeremy Musson and Mary Miers have made many suggestions and Professor Alistair Rowan most generously committed his recollections of his days with the magazine to paper for my benefit.

From *Country Life* I returned to the National Monuments Record of Scotland, all too conscious of how tiresome it must have been for the current staff to have a former colleague demanding to see half-remembered titles; 'I think it is bound in green'. They have coped with great good cheer. The staffs of the National Library, the National Archives of Scotland, particularly Tristram Clark and John McLintock, Hamilton Public Libraries and the Special Collections Department of Aberdeen University Library have all been outstandingly helpful but I want to thank especially the staff of the Scottish Library within Edinburgh Public Libraries, the range and depth of whose choice collections continues to astound me, while those at the Fine Art Library continue to point me in the right direction on an almost daily basis.

At Historic Scotland Dr Richard Fawcett and Aonghus McKechnie have given expert help. For particular help with individual houses I am grateful to Richard Emerson and William Kay, Rosalind Taylor, Ian Scott, Professor Charles McKean, Judith Cripps of Aberdeen City Archives, Dr David Walker, Mary Cosh, Sara Stevenson, James Holloway and Helen Watson of the Scottish National Portrait Gallery, Helen Smailes of the National Galleries of Scotland, Clara Young of Dundee Museums and Art Galleries, Hugh T. Stevenson of Glasgow Museums and Art Galleries,

Adam Swan, James and Ann Simpson, Lorraine Hesketh-Campbell and Craig Fergusson, Nigel Malcolm-Smith and John Gifford. At the National Trust for Scotland both Isla Robertson, Photo Librarian, and Ian Riches, Archivist, have smoothed my path while I am especially indebted to Diana Stevens, Administrator in the Curatorial Department, for her outstanding support and patience in sending the digitised manuscript to Phoebe Clapham, the soundest of editors at Aurum. Kristina Watson at the National Monuments Record of Scotland has masterminded the lengthy photographic order for Aurum with characteristic calmness.

But this book is really about the early days of the National Monuments Record of Scotland. Colin McWilliam died just before we published the *Jubilee Guide* in 1991, but I had the measure of his manifold abilities as a writer, draughtsman and persuader and we dedicated the *Guide* to his memory. Both Christine McWilliam and Professor Sir James Dunbar-Nasmith told me about Colin's party piece lecture on demolished houses. Professor David Walker has read several of the chapters and I am grateful for his profound scholarship. It has been a real pleasure to have this excuse to interview Kitty Cruft about the earliest days on several recent occasions and this book might have been dedicated to her but for the fact that Professor Alistair Rowan and I edited a Festschrift for her, *Scottish Country Houses,* in 1995.

Thus the book is dedicated instead to Jane Thomas, who joined the NMRS to assist with the Travelling Exhibition mounted to mark the Jubilee in 1991. It was my great good fortune that she stayed on to continue the spirit of the Record as an agreeable centre of scholarship after Kitty retired, and one that I have continued to benefit from since I took up the challenge of the Curatorship of the National Trust for Scotland in 1998.

First published in Great Britain
2006 by Aurum Press Ltd
25 Bedford Avenue, London WC1B 3AT

Text copyright © Ian Gow 2006

Ian Gow has asserted his moral right to be identified as the Author of the text of this Work in accordance with the Copyright, Designs and Patents Act 1988.

A catalogue record for this book is available from the British Library.

ISBN 10: 1 84513 051 0

ISBN 13: 978 1 84513 051 0

1 3 5 7 9 10 8 6 4 2
2006 2008 2010 2009 2007

Designed by Peter Ward
Printed and bound in Singapore by CS Graphics

Half-title: Aberdour Castle
Frontispiece: Douglas Castle
Endpapers: Hamilton Palace, ground and first-floor plans

CONTENTS

Introduction

This book is a Scottish companion volume to Giles Worsley's *England's Lost Houses from the Archives of Country Life* (2002). Although Scotland must have lost proportionately quite as many country houses as England, as the Victoria and Albert Museum's arresting and memorable 1974 exhibition *The Destruction of the Country House* demonstrated, the *Country Life* archive could not supply the illustrations for such a book alone.

When *Country Life* turned to Scotland it was to seek out picturesque ancient castles and tower-houses to vary its diet of English country houses, and it would be difficult to overestimate the magazine's impact on the Scots' perception of their own architectural history. Although some tower-houses have been lost, like the handsome Faichfield in Aberdeenshire with its dolls' house version of the Holyroodhouse staterooms, for the most part they have been the subject of a truly remarkable restoration programme, to an extent that there is hardly a single ruined tower-house left in the Scottish landscape other than the carefully managed ancient monuments maintained in a splendid ruination by Historic Scotland.

But *Country Life* did not extend the same affection to nineteenth-century Scotch Baronial castles, which were inspired by the genuine ancient baronial houses but condemned as phoney, sham and smacking of 'Balmorality'. It is these houses, frequently built around an earlier 'genuine' castle, and often very beautiful to us today, that form the majority of twentieth-century losses.

To display these houses in their prime, one has to turn to the National Monuments Record of Scotland, founded in 1941 to survey Scotland's historic architecture in the face of its potential destruction by enemy action. Although it might have been supposed that the Record's task would cease with peacetime, the end of the Second World War heralded a reconstruction boom, and the Record soon found itself no less busily trying to record the nation's historic buildings in the face of different but no less real threats to their existence.

The Record was transformed in 1951 by the appointment of Colin McWilliam, a young English architect. His background was seen as a strength in pursuing the Record's continuing purpose of building up a comprehensive archive of measured drawings, but it soon became obvious, in the face of the sheer scale of demolition during the early 1950s, that only photography could answer. He had already demonstrated a considerable talent as an illustrator, but his eye also made him an inspired photographer. McWilliam's photographs are still instantly recognisable today through their sparkling flair. Nobody else would have

The East Front of Logan House, designed by David Bryce in 1874 in the Scotch Baronial style and demolished in 1952 to reveal the earlier 18th-century house at its core (see p. 15)

Above: Dunmore Park with school desks during requisitioning, 1955
Above right: A school dormitory during requisitioning at Minto, 1956

photographed from inside a four-poster bed as at Newton Don; bothered to record the table set for a frugal lunch with a reduced staff and an electric hot-plate standing by at Fettercairn; captured an untouched nineteenth-century bedroom at Corehouse with ewer and basins, and a slop pail, or taken a photograph of both the exterior and inside of a charming gabled Victorian dolls' house with all its original wallpapers at Maxwellton. He was also a gifted writer, which made him an inspired campaigner in many battles to save Scotland's historic buildings.

At the Record he joined the newly graduated Kitty Cruft, who had been taken on part-time to carry on its day-to-day administration, but was soon out in the field with her trusted Leica camera. Sadly Colin McWilliam died in 1991, just as we were hoping to record his memories for a fiftieth-anniversary publication about the Record's history, but Kitty Cruft still has a very clear recall of these early days.

Their photographs capture the Scottish country house as it emerged from the dreary era of requisitioning, with what looks like Supplies Division chart tables lingering at Craigend Castle; school desks carved with the names of bored juveniles in the corridors of Dunmore Park; white-painted iron cots with neatly folded quilts under an exotic Chinese wallpaper in the temporary school dormitory at Minto; and an abandoned cart and 'Louis' chandelier stacked in William Burn's grand ducal corridor at the Duke of Montrose's abandoned Buchanan Castle after its owners had withdrawn to the Duchess's inherited Hamilton castle at Brodick on the Island of Arran.

When asked if it was not dispiriting to see such once fine buildings in such a sorry state, Kitty remembered the shock of turning up at Archerfield, expecting to see some trace of the finest late-Adam interiors in Scotland, only to find it had just been completely gutted to house grain silos. Some country houses can be seen slipping into a decline over several years in the Record's files, and Kitty photographed Polmaise on the day of the viewing for the 1956 sale of its contents with dealers' cars lined up at the door; the library books neatly divided into lots and ghostly punters inspecting the goods. These are followed in the Record's files by a 1966 press cutting announcing that Polmaise was to be blown up at 10.30 a.m. on 14 July. Polmaise, of course, was a classic unwanted Scotch Baronial pile. One of Colin McWilliam's strengths was that, unlike native Scots, he had not been brought up to despise and reject the Scotch Baronial style, and he brought a fresh and sympathetic eye to Victorian architecture.

There are very few photographs of buildings actually being demolished (see Chapter 1). This gap, however, is amply filled by the papers of Charles Brand, a Dundee demolition contractor whose enthusiasm for his task shines through his photographs and press cuttings, most notably in his blow-by-blow record of Murthly's violent demise (Chapter 16). Just

occasionally the Record staff were called back to record an exciting discovery during demolition, and thus Colin McWilliam recorded a suave Louis XVI Revival Library at Glenormiston in 1956, which looks like the work of Morisons of Edinburgh, while Kitty remembers going back in a snowstorm to record the Watteau-esque painted decorations that came to light when the bookcases had been removed.

One of the most difficult challenges for the record's staff was to ascertain which buildings were currently at threat, and here the Council Members played a vital role in providing a bush telegraph of landowners and architects. Kitty especially remembers being directed to Mertoun in the Borders by Ian G. Lindsay, whose architectural practice was busy reducing this much-extended country house to its original Brucian classic proportions for the Duke of Sutherland in 1953. Kitty thus arrived in time to capture the demolition scene with a site hut, a bath on the lawn, newly removed sash-window frames resting neatly against the walls and carefully stacked stone piled on all sides awaiting transport and re-use.

But there was far too much to record for only two people to cope with and soon Colin McWilliam had recruited a young student, David Walker, already a gifted architectural illustrator, to record his native Dundee. It is a pity, but inevitable, that there are so few records of these three pioneer architectural historians at work, but they were always holding and

ABOVE, LEFT AND BELOW: The Scotch Baronial Polmaise, designed by William Burn in 1863 and photographed by Kitty Cruft during the viewing for the sale of its contents in 1956, with the dealers' cars parked outside. Polmaise was blown up in 1956

RIGHT: David Walker
unwittingly photographing
himself in a sideboard
mirror at Castleroy, 1954

CENTRE: Record
photograph of Old
Balmoral Castle by George
Washington Wilson, c.1854

aiming the camera and usually working alone. Happily, Colin McWilliam unwittingly just caught himself in a mirror in 1956 at Guthrie Castle, Angus; David Walker also recorded his young self while photographing a mirrored sideboard at Castleroy, Broughty Ferry in 1954; while one of the very few photographs in the Record of Kitty Cruft came about when she was asked to stand next to a historic apple tree in 1968 'to give scale' in the walled garden at Crichton House in Midlothian by Priscilla Minay, Librarian of the City of Edinburgh's Fine Art Library, who had a particular interest in the new subject of Garden History.

Colin McWilliam became a redoubtable and highly articulate campaigner in the cause of preserving Scotland's historic buildings, and in 1957 he left the Record to work for the National Trust for Scotland in 1957 as its architectural adviser; in his spare time he led the casework of the Scottish Georgian Society, founded under the inspiring leadership of Eleanor Robertson in 1956. He developed a party-piece lecture providing an outline of Scottish architectural history through slides of key representative buildings, only at the end revealing to the audience that they had all been demolished in the recent past.

Even when its main focus was on survey drawings, the Record placed a high value on historic photography, building up a good collection of early photographically illustrated books. Scotland had been a cradle for photographic experiment through the work of Hill and Adamson and their fellow pioneers. Ancient abbeys and castles, unlike human subjects, were conveniently immobile and had been accepted as appealing picturesque subject matter by more than one recent generation of artists, at a time when Sir Walter Scott's novels held everyone in thrall. Hill and Adamson's principal contribution to lost-house photography was their 1844 Merchiston Castle, Edinburgh, in fact taken to record the school then occupying the building, and showing its pleasant Georgian wings, sheared off in 1961 to restore the integrity of the original tower-house core. An isolated, but sadly unprovenanced, example in the Record of early threatened-building recording is the photograph of the gate of Aberdour Castle, with its top-hatted servants giving scale, moved to accommodate the railway in 1872–3 (see frontispiece).

Photographs of building sites are also rare. One of the earliest surviving is of Dunbeath, showing the original tower-house under repair. Exceptionally, however, Queen Victoria and Prince Albert retained

the Aberdeen photographer George Washington Wilson, then in partnership as Wilson and Hay, to record the building of the new Balmoral Castle in 1853–4 so that they could follow its progress when not in residence. Wilson was also asked to record Old Balmoral Castle, which was ultimately demolished as part of their rebuilding scheme. The Queen literally made Wilson's fortune, as he seems to have been permitted to publish some of his photographs of the royal family's return to their new home in the land of the Queen's Stuart ancestors, and even a surprisingly intrusive interior of the drawing room soon found its way into tourist albums.

The most remarkable of pioneer architect-photographers was unquestionably Charles Kinnear, of the leading Edinburgh architectural partnership Peddie and Kinnear, whose wealth enabled him to pursue photography as a hobby. His architectural and photographic interests came together when he began to make a series of 'before' and 'after' photographs of their commissions. Drygrange House *c.* 1888 is an excellent example, with photographs taken from exactly the same spot allowing one to trace a conti-nuity in the trees when so much else had changed. These photographs had a seductive commercial value alongside the record making, because they demon-

strated his skills to potential clients and gave them the confidence to replace an old house with a new one.

Very few patrons had Kinnear's sense of history, although many photographers were commissioned by proud owners to make photographic studies of newly built or altered houses in the established British tradition of creating albums of watercolours. A series of photographs of Philiphaugh House, in Selkirkshire, by the local photographer, Clapperton, bear inscriptions to show that they record the appearance of the house 'before Mr. Steel made his

ABOVE: Before and after photographs of Drygrange House taken by its architect, Charles Kinnear, *c.*1889

alterations', and the nature of photographic reproduction made limited editions of such surveys possible, as the topographical publications by Annan of Glasgow make clear.

In a few fortunate cases a lost house can be revisited through the surviving negatives of a local photographer. The outstanding collection is that of Magnus Jackson of Perth, whose patrons employed him to record their newly aggrandised and often Scotch Baronialised seats in an area of Scotland that was to be particularly affected in the twentieth century by wholesale demolition of these now deeply unfashionable houses. Most notably he enjoyed the patronage of the Earl of Mansfield, who had retained him in 1893 to make a record in 250 plates of the outstanding art collections at Scone Palace. His photographs, which include several of Murthly (Chapter 16), deserve a book to themselves.

In contrast to this specialist kind of record, many now lost houses were rather more randomly captured by the tourist photography that mushroomed in the wake of Scotland's new-found popularity. Local shopkeepers, particularly chemists, kept prints of attractions including historic buildings and big houses for purchase by tourists, and postcards were produced by the same method for sale by hotels and boarding houses. Because of this blanket local coverage to appeal to all tastes, many otherwise conventionally un-picturesque houses were recorded for posterity.

As a measure of the low esteem in which the Scotch Baronial style was held until comparatively recent times, when the Threave Estate came to The National Trust for Scotland in 1948, the donor, Major A.F. Gordon, offered to blow up the House, built by Peddie and Kinnear for his grandfather in 1871, to make his gift more palatable. It happily survived because the Trust set up a School of Practical Gardening, using the House as the classrooms and dormitories, and over half a century later it is open to the public with its original furnishings. Now regarded as a masterpiece, it is a prime attraction for visitors to the estate, with a particularly thrilling staircase rising through six floors.

This anecdote reflects the wider sea-change in public and official attitudes towards the conservation of historic houses, which can be easily traced over the period covered in this book. Robert Adam's Balbardie functioned as a decayed tenement building for several decades before the demolition of most of the structure in 1956; the lovely Palladian villa of Seaton, which passed into the hands of Aberdeen City Council in 1956, lay empty until vandals set it on fire in 1963. John Adam's Hawkhill, on the outskirts of Edinburgh, also met its end at the hands of vandals, in 1972, but the Scottish Georgian Society succeeded in saving the handsome cycle of decorative paintings in the dining room, and within the next few years the tide of opinion turned in favour of the conservationists.

This is not to say that there are no longer any threats to Scotland's architectural heritage. Fire has always been a major cause of country-house losses, and remains so today, although recently there have been enormous advances in protective technology and rapid response times. The chronological sequences of photographs in the National Monuments Record of many country houses that became hotels make apparent that all too many ended as fire-blackened ruins. The archetype of this type of loss is Montgomerie House in Ayrshire (see appendix), a beautiful neo-classical house built by the architect John Paterson in 1804. Gutted by fire in April 1968, it was demolished by July 1969, its sorry fate encapsulated by Colin McWilliam in a pair of particularly memorable 'before' and 'after' photographs taken from the same viewpoint.

In the wake of the grievous fires at Hampton Court, Uppark and Windsor, some important buildings including the Palace of Holyroodhouse have been photographically recorded in intensive detail. The National Trust for Scotland has been luckier than its older sister, the National Trust, which has had to bear the tragic loss of Coleshill, but it seemed worth highlighting in this book how nearly we lost Crathes, with its exceptionally fine painted ceilings and rare early oak furniture.

Responses to fires have varied with the ages. Fires in the past were viewed much more as

Milton Lockhart House, designed by William Burn in 1829 and photographed before its demolition and subsequent rebuilding in Japan.

architectural opportunities than they are in our conservation-minded days. The fires at Douglas Castle and Rosneath in 1758 and 1802 respectively facilitated two particularly innovative buildings. Sir Robert Lorimer's architectural practice in the early twentieth century specialised in reinstating fire-damaged structures, to the extent that Lorimer was not shy of telegraphing distressed owners in the aftermath of fires. Monzie and, on an even larger scale, Dunrobin were classic examples of Lorimer's post-fire reinstatement exercises. The plasterers Grandisons, based in Peebles, are another Scottish firm who seem to have developed their reputation on the strength of their outstanding skills in reinstating fire-damaged plasterwork in both Scotland and the North of England.

Although it does not mitigate a grievous tragedy, the swift rebuilding of Inveraray Castle after the very serious fire on 5 November 1975 reflected a turning point in attitudes to preservation, and inspired the conservation of further houses. The success of Inveraray's rebuilding owed everything to the prompt action of the late Duke of Argyll and his architects, Ian G. Lindsay and Partners, who had worked on its restoration twenty-five years before and who immediately drilled holes in the magnificent neo-classical plasterwork of Mylne's ceilings to prevent their collapse under the weight of the water from the firemen's hoses.

Mar Lodge, which came to The National Trust for Scotland in 1995 after a serious fire and an insurance reinstatement rebuilding project, is also an interesting case study as it is not only open to the public several days a year, but is now also enjoying a new lease of life as holiday apartments. It was built for the Duke and Duchess of Fife in 1895 to the designs of A. Marshall Mackenzie and the foundation stone was laid by Queen Victoria, the Duchess's grandmother. Designed as a shooting lodge, rather than a Scotch Baronial castle, both the interior and exterior had a wealth of exposed timber and panelling with a staircase at the centre of the butterfly plan and, since the fire broke out during a renovation when all the timber doors were in store, the centre of the house was lost in the conflagration but the distant ends of the wings largely escaped. Mercifully, many of the contents, including a superlative run of mounted stags' heads dating back to 1797, were carefully stored in the detached ballroom and thus escaped destruction, contributing a great deal to the character of the rebuilt house, which is a great tribute to modern architectural and craft skills.

It must be remembered, of course, that not all lost houses are wholly vanished. The transportation difficulties and challenges inherent in the very geography of Scotland put a premium on any materials that were to hand, and building materials have always had a resale value, something that emerges clearly from the records of Charles Brand of Dundee. The demolition of Hamilton Palace occurred in 1919, when many of its components like the large areas of historic carved oak panelling had a resale value on the antique market, particularly in America, and the Hamilton Estate were well satisfied, as contemporary newspaper accounts attest, with the prices obtained at this great house-breaking auction, although it is perhaps no surprise to learn that the great Imperial staircase, in the Duke's favourite black marble, failed to find an immediate purchaser.

Thus Hamilton Palace is far from lost and continues to be found. Large areas of balustrade and ornamental stonework went to enrich the nearby terrace gardens at Barncluith; the Great Dining Room was reconstructed in the Museum of the Fine Arts, Boston and now supplies a magnificent, and appropriate, background to their outstanding collections of silver, while the National Museums of Scotland recently brought back from America the components of the Drawing Room, which had remained in their packing cases during their sojourn in America.

Perhaps the ultimate act of salvage, and one that has done much to mitigate the gloom inspired by this litany of demolition, has been the popularity in Scotland of excavating out of a distended nineteenth-century pile the much smaller historic core, whose diminutive scale is better suited to a simpler way of life without staff. The most spectacularly successful example of this is Logan House in Wigtonshire. This was probably enormously influential in Scotland as a result of a feature on it in *Country Life* by Christopher Hussey on 5 August 1954 – a particularly dark period for country-house losses. There is a Mary Poppins quality about the apparent ease with which this time-lapse photography shows how a particularly ugly Scotch Baronial duckling, or turkey, was taken back to become the prettiest of cygnets. Nobody was more able than Hussey to put the Logan experience into the wider British context and to pass on the thrill of how the old house was revealed after being totally and invisibly immured in the 'dour' and 'Victorian baronial mansion', correctly attributed to Bryce. Just as nothing could have been more unfashionable in 1954 than the Bryce house of 1874, so nothing could have been more in tune with

contemporary taste than the neat and quiet early Georgian house with the prettiest of panelled rooms and a dream of a miniature sweeping stair. Not surprisingly this outstanding success inspired the owners of many local country houses like nearby Ardwell to follow suit. Colin McWilliam recorded the Baronial Ardwell in 1956 at the onset of this drastic slimming down programme, with its evocative lines of heraldic pennants still fluttering in the vast stairhall with its barley-sugar banisters below an elegant cove with particularly lively and light decorative painting. The ruins of Milton Lockhart House in Lanarkshire, designed by William Burn in 1829, were salvaged by being exported stone by stone to Japan, where there is a particular respect for stone buildings, to form the focus of a Santa Claus theme park under the careful supervision of the Edinburgh architects Stewart Tod and partners.

A word of explanation may be needed for the selection of this particular grouping of houses when the pool is so large. *Country Life* remains the starting point with Brahan Castle, one of the saddest losses of a great Highland treasure house. I had already extensively published the *Country Life* survey of Hamilton Palace in *Scottish Houses and Gardens* (1997) and this book gave the opportunity to look at the other photographic records of Scotland's greatest country house and the most grievous loss of all. Dunglass owes its modern celebrity almost solely to Christopher Hussey's 1925 article, and both Abercairney and Millearne show how a younger generation of writers at the magazine took up the cause of these unfashionable nineteenth-century houses.

It was natural that the next call would be the National Monuments Record of Scotland, and the focus thus inevitably turned from the perfected photographic images that were the lifeblood of *Country Life* to the demolitions that formed the grim preoccupation of its lively young staff in the early 1950s. The Record also acted as central depot for collecting and copying earlier photographic images of vanished houses, and from these Amisfield is the outstanding example. Another highlight of the Record must be the Charles Brand Collection,

reflecting his long and successful career as demolition agent to the gentry, best represented by his remarkable record of Murthly's demise.

The great Scottish Houses were self-selecting, with Douglas and Gordon Castles topping any list, while sorry Panmure has left a memory of a Romantic past. I trawled through the 10,000 boxes of photographic prints in pursuit of the remaining houses and inevitably my selection will be seen as arbitrary. I had remembered Seaton as a particularly magical house and it seemed important to highlight the fate of villas caught up in various degrees of urban expansion, and thus Kelvingrove and Hawkhill followed.

Old House of Hedderwick was canvassed by Richard Emerson, Chief Inspector of Historic Buildings for Scotland, who was the first to connect its stuccowork with that of Ezer at nearby House of Dun. Rosneath has a similar architectural history to Dunglass, with in addition an outstandingly poignant photographic portfolio and the interest of having been deemed 'unsaveable' in 1961, although it is the house that, had it survived, one would most like to visit – after, of course, Hamilton Palace.

Although Robert Adam is generally regarded as

Scotland's most celebrated architect who enjoys an international reputation, his executed works have not always been cherished by the Scots. Balbardie stands as a representative example of one of his houses which fell on hard times and whose outstanding beauty has the additional interest of inspiring an early recording zeal.

Carbet Castle represents the mushrooming of industrialists' new houses with the new wealth generated by Victorian Scotland, and like so many houses soon fell in the popular esteem. Fintray is a good example of a sacrificial house that allowed the preservation of an architectural gem, in its case Craigievar, one of the best loved of all Scottish tower-houses. Guisachan was intimately linked with Haddo, which preserves the most important cycle of interior decoration in the care of The National Trust for Scotland. As a reminder of the threat that fire still poses to the built heritage, Crathes is the supreme Trust example of how pernicious this danger remains, with its capacity for destroying in a few hours the carefully perfected vision derived from centuries of effort. But Mavisbank, which is far from being a Lost House, brings the hope that even the sorriest-looking ruins can be brought back to life and given a significant purpose.

Ian Gow
Edinburgh
March 2006

The exterior and interior of Logan House, after the reinstatement of the Georgian core following the demolition of the Scotch Baronial entrance front, designed by Bryce and demolished in 1954

ABOVE: Wishaw House
during demolition, 1953

RIGHT AND BELOW:
Westerhall during
demolition, 1955

LEFT: Centrepiece of James
Smith's South Front of
Hamilton Palace during the
demolition, c. 1925

CHAPTER ONE

A Portfolio of Decay and Demolition

Although demolition was such a preoccupation of the Scottish National Buildings Record during the early 1950s, there are surprisingly few photographs of demolition sites. The inspiration for the Record was primarily aesthetic and perhaps the act of demolition was seen as a failure to record a building in time and thus a battle lost. Just as this book was going to press, however, a published photograph of the demolition of Hamilton Palace, perhaps the most celebrated demolition in Scottish architectural history, came to light in the Royal Incorporation of Architects in *Scotland's Quarterly* for 1925. Although the focus remains the grand Palladian architecture of James Smith's pedimented frontispiece, the left foreground shows some of the massive braced timber machinery used to level the once proud palace with the dust.

Perhaps the archetypal Record photograph of a demolition site is Colin McWilliam's 1953 photograph of Wishaw House, in Lanarkshire, which is starkly un-picturesque. According to Groome's *Ordnance Gazetteer of Scotland* (1901), Wishaw House had been enlarged and improved by James Gillespie Graham before 1839, and enough castellated detail survives in the photograph to make this seem convincing. There is an absolutely classic site hut on the far left, and a sense of order with the valuable timber stacked up neatly, and an impression that the walls were being carefully dismantled to extract the timbers without damage.

By contrast, Colin McWilliam's 1955 photographs of the demolition of Westerhall, in Dumfriesshire, are surprisingly low-tech, with the workmen grubbing the walls away with brute force and a sense of untidy disorder. It was very unusual for such an attractive small tower-house to be demolished but Groome says that Westerhall had been restored following 'great damage by fire in Feb. 1873' and perhaps had lost some of its charm in the extensive rebuilding. The photograph of the stair hall, with its striking wallpaper, shows how the timbers have been neatly sawn through, but it seems careless that nobody had bothered to salvage the chandelier. Both of these records seem characteristic of Colin McWilliam's remarkable eye, and few other people would have bothered to make such a record at the eleventh hour.

A memorable modern demolition-site photograph is the NMRS photograph of Minto House from 1993, with just an angle of walls standing and a caterpillar vehicle raised high on a great mountain of spoil reducing what was left, with a lorry ready to take this discarded material away. Similar, though of a villa rather than a country house, is the 1994 photograph of 89 Eldon Street, Greenock, with this handsome stone-built Victorian villa with bay windows completely obscured

ABOVE: A fine neo-classical domed interior at Dreghorn reduced to frass, 1955

RIGHT: Beheaded caryatids from a demolished chimney-piece at Dreghorn, parked on a cast-iron balcony, 1955

attractive castellated Edinburgh villa, with elegant Soanic-detailed classical interiors, with fine plaster-work and chimney-pieces, in the photographs taken by Colin McWilliam in 1955 it looks as though it has been shredded. There is no written explanation of its state but on being shown the photographs after fifty years, Kitty Cruft immediately explained, 'You have to understand that it stood on army land and was used for target practice!' The survey culminates in a photograph which has just the suspicion of having been art-directed by Colin McWilliam, with two discarded caryatid fragments of a once noble chimney-piece posed on either side of the balcony of one of the circular headed windows. The exterior photographs include a poster warning 'DANGER' but sadly the rest is illegible.

Close second to Dreghorn, but with a touch of surrealism, come George Nichol's 1965 photographs of Kennet House. This handsome neo-classical house, designed by Thomas Harrison in 1793, was captured at a low ebb by Nichol, one of the most talented photographers ever to work for the Record. His view of the façade could not avoid an off-centre corrugated-iron garage where all was otherwise good taste and symmetry. Indoors, a dustbin is posed at a jaunty angle in an exquisite Doric-composition fireplace with Cupid disporting himself on the tablet; old deckchairs, forks and shovels, buckets and sacks fill the drawing rooms and the only surviving furnishing is a stuffed stag's head still lording it over the elegant staircase with its glassy stare – presumably because it was too high up to be readily removable. Kennet was not to suffer such indignities for long as it was demolished in March 1967.

Not all ruins are photogenic and vegetation, with a long period of gestation as in the remains of a border abbey, is perhaps the key component for visual pleasure. The photographs of Midhope Castle on the Hopetoun Estate, taken over several years, have enough Brucian detail in the disintegrating panelling to give one a sense that architectural order could still – with a great deal of effort – be recovered, as well as a painted ceiling coming to light as the damp plaster obeyed the force of gravity. Distinctly creepy photographic surveys of ruins

by a sinister mass of monkey-puzzle trees, one gate-pier away to facilitate the entry of lorries and an enormous sign-board advertising the named 'Builders & Demolishers' with a phone number.

There can be no dispute as to winner of the photographic survey of the most grievously damaged building; nothing in the Record can rival the wreckage of Dreghorn Castle in Edinburgh. Once an

include Colin McWilliam's photographs of Lindertis from 1956 and the photographer from the Ministry of Works' survey of Rossie Castle, completely gutted out internally, but with the main façades still in place and the wings ending in Piranesian heaps of masonry.

The idea of this portfolio was suggested by John Harris, one of the organisers of the 1974 *Destruction of the Country House* exhibition at the Victoria and Albert Museum, and it seems sensible to end with a particular category of photograph – the press photo-opportunity. The favourite photo-opportunities are principally provided by two circumstances – fire and explosives. The classic and deeply tragic country-house fire photograph is the much-reproduced study of Penicuik on the morning after 16 June 1899 with the furniture and pictures stacked on the lawn after their heroic rescue by the staff and tenantry; but they could do nothing to save the great Alexander Runciman eighteenth-century painted ceiling of 'Ossian's Hall', perhaps the first Scotch Baronial interior in Scotland. There are detailed accounts of this slow-burning but disastrous fire in the local press; it 'differed from ordinary ones in that there was no grand culminating point marked by the falling in of the main roof or the collapse of outer walls. Rather did it resemble a hand-to-hand encounter with a determined enemy in a fortress, where it would take hours to decide the victory.' These accounts were used to brilliant effect by Alistair Rowan in *Country Life* on 15 August 1968. (After more than a century, there are now plans to consolidate Penicuik as a ruin and open it to the public.) A real press photograph is a similar study of the 1915 destruction of Philorth, 'totally destroyed by fire', though sadly with less well-furnished lawns.

In their follow-up to the 1974 exhibition, *Lost Houses of Scotland* (1980), published by Save Britain's Heritage, Marcus Binney and John Harris were struck by the uniquely Scottish predilection for dynamiting houses. The *Scotsman* newspaper was an avid publisher of the genre with a particularly memorable study of Rosneath (page 122). Even more striking are the blow-by-blow photographs of Murthly's demise, proudly taken by the demolition contractor and reproduced on pages 141–5.

ABOVE: The morning after the fire at Penicuik House in 1899 with salvaged plenishings on the lawn

LEFT: The interior of Midhope Tower on the Hopetoun Estate in extreme decay

BELOW: The still smouldering ruins of Philorth House in 1915, with salvaged furnishings

CHAPTER TWO

Mavisbank:
Endangered not Lost

Midlothian

PIONEERING SUBURBAN VILLA
WITH DETAILING BY WILLIAM ADAM

In 1980, only six years after their exhibition *The Destruction of the Country House* at the Victoria and Albert Museum, Marcus Binney and John Harris came to Scotland to research their *Lost Houses of Scotland*, published by Save Britain's Heritage. Working from the county lists of houses destroyed in England, Scotland and Wales drawn up by the National Monuments Records for the earlier exhibition, they visited the sites of all the Scottish houses listed and came to a series of thoughtful conclusions that were often at odds with the apocalyptic vision presented in the 1974 exhibition. Although many houses had indeed vanished, their survey revealed that not only were many still happily standing as often picturesque ruins, but that, as a result of the Scottish tradition of building soundly in stone, they were not necessarily deteriorating. Binney and Harris were surprised to discover that offices and ancillary buildings had frequently survived the loss of a house, and that many estates and parklands were still beautiful places.

Where a house survives in Scotland, there is always a chance of rescue, even at the eleventh hour. This was to be the theme of Marcus Dean and Mary Meirs' *Scotland's Endangered Houses*, also published by SAVE in 1990, which is very much a D.I.Y. manual on how to rescue an endangered house. Taken together, these SAVE publications represent a definitive change of mood and a radically different climate from the attitudes that the Scottish National Buildings Record grappled with during the 1950s.

Mavisbank's emergence as the *cause célèbre* of the Scottish conservation movement owes much to the Record's arresting 1973 photograph, taken in the aftermath of a fire. Mavisbank was designed in 1723 by Sir John Clerk of Penicuik, an amateur of architecture, as a pioneering suburban villa, with the practical details being left to William Adam. In spite of the foreground of dereliction, the sheer quality and diminutive grace of the ruin rising above seems to deliver a profound and powerful message: 'Save me!' A great strength of Binney and Harris's *Lost Houses* is that they include brief descriptive notes on each site they

TOP: Mavisbank at its lowest ebb after the fire in 1973, with the courtyard filled with wrecked cars

LEFT: Two early Victorian photographs of Mavisbank in its bucolic prime, *c.* 1870

visited and their account of Mavisbank takes a perhaps surprisingly optimistic line as they succumbed
to the ruin's charms, in spite of the all too obvious
drawbacks:

> Ruin, beautiful rising from trash heap. Caravans
> and wrecked cars now parked in front of house.
> Shell though suffering from some subsidence,
> survives to remarkable extent – with very fine
> carved detail. Despite proximity to Edinburgh,
> house is marvellously secluded – approached
> down a winding chestnut drive. Main front looks
> out over parkland and small lake. Behind ground
> rises sharply with banks of rhododendrons.

A quarter of a century later this optimism is
widely shared and there seems a real likelihood that,
far from mourning the loss of Mavisbank in the near
future, we will be able to enjoy a walk through the
rooms of its piano nobile and enjoy the views over its
attractive setting. The house made an appearance in
BBC2's *Restoration* series in 2003, garnering much-

needed publicity though failing to win the prize of
funds for restoration. Now Historic Scotland is very
much on the case and the Mavisbank Trust is
currently researching the possibilities.

Mavisbank has the good fortune to be exceptionally well documented in the Clerk of Penicuik
muniments. The set of engraved plans are unusually
bucolic, accompanied by an elevation with foliage
glimpsed through the arcaded quadrants that
embrace its forecourt, showing its highly decorated
architecture with carved festoons and vases rising to
its convex domed roof, like a Baroque bracket clock.

The villa's salvation has also been promoted by
the biographical researches of Dr Iain G. Brown and
others on Sir John Clerk and his historical milieu,
which supply the context for this enchanting villa and
deepen our understanding of its genesis. The house
was built to show off Sir John's art collection, which
has also been the subject of further research, with
many of its treasures being traced. One of Sir John's
justifications for this extravagance, which might

have been more wisely invested in the Clerks' seat at Penicuik, to the south of Edinburgh, was that frequent, if temporary, residence at Mavisbank would facilitate supervision of the family's coal-mining interests in its vicinity. By great good fortune, Sir John and William Adam built the villa exceptionally strongly to withstand mineral extraction in the ground below, and the Coal Board put this to the test.

Like many villas, Mavisbank was perfectly tailored to Sir John's needs, and inevitably later generations of the family found it less suitable, selling the building and removing the art collections to Penicuik House. But such a pretty house in such an attractive and convenient setting was never short of admiring owners, who continued to make improvements. During the late nineteenth century it was acquired for a lunatic asylum, whose inmates were intended to benefit from its country air and restful scenery; this project was so successful that the villa was soon lost in mushrooming extensions. But Mavisbank's Early Georgian charm was still sufficient

for a private owner in 1954 to commission the architect Robert Hurd to remove these excrescences and return it to its original diminutive size; these efforts can now be studied in Hurd's office files in the National Monuments Record of Scotland.

Sadly, these promising beginnings were followed by a period of misfortune, with complications of ownership resulting in a spell as a caravan site and car dump, culminating in the grievous fire in 1973. Fortunately, in 1954 Colin McWilliam had taken some crucial record photographs of interior details including Calderwood's plasterwork of the cove over the Great Staircase, and William Adam's marble chimney-pieces for the Great Dining Room, and the Best Bedroom, the latter framing an over-mantel mirror. It seems almost certain that archaeological excavation will reveal further interior detail.

Further discoveries have been made in the intervening years. The Record's 1973 post-fire photographic survey reveals the sheer quality of the richly undercut stone-carving by John Silverstyn, with

FROM FAR LEFT: the Great Dining Room chimney-piece by William Adam; the cornice and cove over the Great Staircase with plasterwork by Calderwood; William Adam's Best Bedroom chimney-piece with his modish integral marble-framed chimney-glass

LEFT: Detail of John Silverstyn's exceptionally high-quality carved ornaments, 1973

OPPOSITE: Early Victorian photograph of the drawing room at Mavisbank with its new furniture supplied by Charles Trotter of Edinburgh

heraldic detail originally tinctured with colour. There was great excitement in 1987 when some early photographs of the villa in the days before the lunatic asylum, discovered in a private collection, revealed not just the detail of the domed roof but also how nobly it commanded its little landscaped valley and brought it to life with smoking chimneys. At some point in the second quarter of the nineteenth century, possibly in 1842 when George Clerk Arbuthnot acquired the villa from Graeme Mercer, its owner brought the piano nobile down to ground-floor level and ingeniously added large rooms behind the wings without impairing Sir John and William Adam's design. Then by further good fortune a photograph of the interior of its new drawing room was identified in an album that had been acquired by the National Monuments Record of Scotland; even more surprisingly, this photograph allowed a design elevation of the drawing room to be identified in the NMRS's albums of drawings by Trotters, the Edinburgh cabinet-makers and upholsters.

Thus, rather in the reverse of the process followed in the other chapters of this book, where an understanding of a lost house is deepened as each new visual record is discovered, here the visual records will directly inform the eventual restoration of Mavisbank. But this has not come about without a struggle. Although the caravan site and car dump were cleared away in 1986, and I covered the house in a *Country Life* article of 20 August 1987, there was a real fear in 1989 that the ruin would be declared a dangerous building and bulldozed. A vigilante movement to prevent this sprung into action, culminating in the feasibility study that was undertaken by the Lothian Building Preservation Trust in April of that year, which usefully coincided with the William Adam tercentenary celebrations. There can be no doubt that Mavisbank's eventual restoration will encourage other bids to prevent endangered buildings becoming lost houses of Scotland.

CHAPTER THREE

Hamilton Palace

Lanarkshire

THE BIGGEST COUNTRY HOUSE IN SCOTLAND BITES THE DUST IN 1919

Had it not been 'levelled with the dust' in 1919 after the dispersal of its fabled contents to their current places in the great museums throughout the world, Hamilton Palace would still be a prime Scottish tourist destination today, single-handedly creating a very different image from tartanry. It was simply the largest house in Scotland, and it could hold its own proudly against any of the stately homes of England.

Now we can only visit it visually through the medium of the photographic record and we must be grateful for the relatively few photographs that survive. In Hamilton, where the loss is most deeply felt, the local reference library has assiduously gathered together photographs, inventories and plans – many deriving from the Duke of Hamilton's own collections – and kept a memory of this vast Palace alive through the medium of a slim pamphlet, *Hamilton Palace: a photographic record* by G. Walker. The National Monuments Record of Scotland has also been collecting and copying images of the Palace since its foundation in 1941, because any assessment of the surviving stock of Scotland's historic architecture can only be made in the light of what has already been lost.

The Palace was ancient and had been altered and brought up to date by many of Scotland's leading architects, including James Smith, who designed its fine Palladian Corinthian frontispiece during the 1690s, and William Adam in the second quarter of the eighteenth century, who was responsible for a run of splendid staterooms with stuccowork by Clayton. Adam and Clayton were also responsible for the eyecatching silhouette of the Chatelherault Banqueting House and Dog Kennels, which closed the long Baroque vista from the Palace and whose name commemorated the French dukedom that had been conferred upon the family. Complete with one of Scotland's greatest art collections, it was a major tourist attraction even before Alexander, Tenth Duke of Hamilton, who succeeded in 1819, totally transformed it to suit his own taste for princely magnificence.

This magnificence was made possible by the apparently limitless wealth conferred upon the Hamiltons from the Lanarkshire coalfields and their extensive mineral rights. During his travels in Europe, the Duke took full advantage of the

LEFT: Annan's oblique view of the new north front of Hamilton Palace dramatises the monumentality of the Tenth Duke's monolithic portico. On the right is his new office wing, *c.* 1882

redistribution of works of art following the upheaval of the French Revolution and the conquests of his hero, Napoleon. Agents throughout Europe continued to act on the Duke's behalf to the end of his life, by which time the Palace interiors were encrusted with art treasures like some fabulous coral reef. In 1810 the Duke married his cousin Susan Beckford, the younger daughter of William Beckford, one of the greatest art connoisseurs of the age. After Beckford died in Bath in 1844 a great deal of his collection was sent northwards to be incorporated into the already densely packed interiors.

The Tenth Duke was, on the whole, respectful of his inheritance and his new work simply wrapped the one-room-thick open courtyard of the ancient Palace in a colossal embrace, preserving the old kitchen courtyard, to create a massive new front with a monumental freestanding Corinthian portico of monolithic columns. Although the Duke toyed with such leading European architects as Percier, Fontaine and Quarenghi, as Professor Tait has shown in the *Burlington Magazine* for July 1983, much of the new decorative work was entrusted to the London decorator and designer Robert Hume, who had also worked for Beckford, with the Glasgow architect David Hamilton supervising on site.

At the heart of the Palace and lying immediately behind Smith's more modest pedimented frontispiece was the picture gallery, built to show off the existing ducal art collections, which had always overflowed into the old Baroque state apartment down the left-hand wing of the original courtyard. The most famous painting in the original art collection was a Rubens well tuned to accord with the Protestant sensibilities of Scotland, depicting as it did *Daniel in the Lions' Den*. Like so many of the Palace's treasures this has ended up outside Scotland, as one of the highlights of the National Gallery in Washington.

With the benefit of hindsight, it was, perhaps, unfortunate that in order to balance this old work with the splendid new nineteenth-century interiors, the Duke had so much of the old interior work renewed or, as the *New Statistical Account* wrote of the Gallery in 1845, 'thoroughly repaired'. The Baroque stair was remodelled, while the seventeenth-century rooms were given richer fireplaces and new ornamental ceilings, often in *trompe l'oeil*. There was thus little sense in 1919 that Scotland was losing one of its most historic domestic structures, while nothing could be more unfashionable than the Louis Revival excesses of the Duke's new work.

This old work, however, meant the Duke's architect had to provide a great deal of new and suitably monumental circulation space traversing the old walls, whose lighting had often to be indirect. An apparently insuperable oddity of the plan was that the Duke's new Great Hall on the piano nobile did not interconnect axially with the transverse Long Gallery at the centre of the Old Palace and thus the circulation could only be resolved in the offset and top-lit main hall, known as the Tribune, the hub of the house, but a space with all the homeliness of a head-office banking hall; it is little wonder that after the First World War the then Duke preferred the relative modesty of his house at Dungavel instead.

Our chief records of Hamilton Palace in its prime are the glass-plate negatives taken by the Glasgow photo-grapher Thomas Annan. Bound albums of prints are held in the Hamilton Library Collection, presumably the ducal set, but the views published here are taken from the less-familiar album of prints in Glasgow University Library. Nothing is known of the circumstances of Annan's commission but it was probably related to the 1882 sale. The remarkable precision of the Annan photographs can be related to two very extensive manuscript inventories, now in Hamilton Library, showing how these art treasures were disposed in the individual rooms in 1836 and 1876. The earlier inventory is particularly revealing because it shows the Palace in a state of flux, with many features awaiting completion, while new carpets and decorations are carefully dated and appended as they arrived. The earlier inventory has had the lists of Beckford treasures that were being sent up from Bath stitched inside its cover. The 1876 inventory has a valedictory tone, with fulsome provenances trumpeted, but is ruthlessly marked up with pencil instructions for the 1882 sale.

Interior photography had always offered particular challenges, but Annan was at pains to do justice to

these monumental new rooms. An 1883 account in H. Baden-Pritchard's *The Photographic Studios of Europe* of an exhibition of these photographs reveals that they were regarded as technically exceptional and records that Annan used 16" x 13" plates and a Dallmeyer 12" x 10" camera. All these interiors were taken with wet collodion, some of them with nearly an hour's exposure. His finesse is confirmed by the view of the Great Hall. This continued indoors, in fluted pilasters of the same stone and sheer walls of ashlar, the exterior order of the portico's monolithic columns and it is a tribute to Annan's lens that it captured the matching trabeated ceiling high above. This vast space was peopled with bronze statuary on Irish black marble bases polished to such a gloss that they reflected the pavement like a mirror. According

to the 1876 inventory these bronzes had a glamorous provenance, having been 'cast in Italy by order of Francoise Premier early in the sixteenth century for the decoration of his Palace at Villeroi in moulds taken from the original statues'. They were part-nered by a 'colossal bronze bust' of Duke Alexander in the central axial niche opposite the front door where one might have expected, in a more conven-tional plan, a doorcase leading through to the ancient picture gallery. This immense space was lit by the '4 massive ebonised stands 7 feet high with ground Glass Globes for Gas'. There were two matching black-marble fireplaces with '2 massive grates and 2 ditto fenders' surmounted by the Duke's armorial bearings. The door to the left of the right-hand chimney-piece, also with a surround of black marble,

Annan's camera lens visually embraced the majestic height of the fluted Corinthian pilasters which continue the order of the portico

Annan captured the soaring height of the Tribune, the hub of the house, whose gallery, carried on trussed brackets, led to the many bedroom apartments

led, through the first of many interconnecting corridors, to the Tribune which interconnected both the main living rooms on the piano nobile and, by means of its second-floor gallery, the principal guest bedrooms above.

Annan's clever lenses could not hope to record this soaring space for posterity, instead focusing on the fireplace, a 'richly carved chimneypiece brought from Florence' that held an apparently appropriate 'Gothic stove'. An unusual characteristic of all Duke Alexander's rooms was that their carpets were made exactly to fit, and this 'Large Turkey Carpet' was no exception. A separate detail photograph in the Glasgow album is devoted to the side wall, on which was displayed Winterhalter's portrait of Princess Marie of Baden, in 1876 the Duchess of Hamilton.

She was hung dynastically above the bust of her cousin Louis Napoleon, and the room also contained busts of Napoleon the First and Second. The bust of Louis Napoleon stood on one of a pair of 'fine Egyptian grey granite stands on fine massive standards' of white marble 'sculptured to represent dolphins on black wood plinths'. In the centre of the room is one of a pair of gilt-bronze tables, made in Paris in 1823 to support exceptionally large slabs of porphyry, that are now in the Art Gallery of Ontario, Canada.

One of the doors beside the chimney-piece led through into the library, the principal living room of the Palace. This was christened the 'Hamilton Library' to distinguish it from the new 'Beckford Library', which had to be ingeniously shoe-horned in by Beckford's architect, H.E. Goodrich, when the Duchess inherited her late father's possessions. In the library the Tribune door was ingeniously fitted into the arcade of bookcases, paced out by pilasters, that ran around the room, and it must have been a jib door with dummy books. The doors to the book-cases were extravagant single sheets of plate glass, unbroken by astragals. It is difficult to assign a style, other than Monumental Classic, to this handsome library, whose trabeated ceiling was caught in Annan's lens, along with one of his camera tripods, at the end of the enfilade through the lined-up doorways. This room had a massive chimney-piece 'of Egyptian porphyry' and it is an oddity of the

The library, with its crimson damask upholstery, was intended as the most comfortable of the state rooms but was no less sumptuous than the others, with a porphyry chimney-piece, rock-crystal chandelier and plate-glass doors protecting the outstanding collection of books

Hamilton inventories, but one which hauntingly prefigures the demolition sale catalogue, that these architectural elements, normally considered fixtures, are included as separate items; this chimney-piece is now in the hall of the National Trust's Hinton Ampner in Hampshire. The mantel clock was in gilt metal with figures of 'Venus and Cupid under a glass shade' and '2 bronze gilt candleabra on bronze vases', which had previously 'belonged to Marie Antoinette Queen of France'. The fitted carpet which ran through these rooms bore the Hamilton cinquefoil in 'black and white' on a crimson ground, according to the 1919 sale catalogue. Just visible behind the sofa to the left of the fireplace was 'An inlaid Mahogany Writing Table ornamented with Gilt Bronze . . . From the Duc de Choiseuls'. This essential piece of library furniture was pushed to one side by the '12 Ebonised chairs, Seats Backs covered in Crimson Damask fringes etc . . . 2 Large sofas to match' surrounding the central square table, demonstrating that this room was conceived as a sitting room, although a sombre one. Professor Waagen, Director of the Royal Gallery of Pictures in Berlin, commented following his visit to the Palace:

> As the Duke combined in equal measure a
> love of art with a love of splendour and was an
> especial lover of beautiful and rare marbles the
> whole ameublement was on a scale of costliness
> with a more numerous display of tables and
> cabinets of the richest Florentine mosaic than I
> had seen in any other palace. As a full crimson
> predominated in the carpets, a deep brown in
> the woods of the furniture, and a black Irish
> marble, as deep in colour as the nero antico, in
> the specimens of marble, the general effect was
> that of the most massive and truly princely
> splendour; at the same time somewhat gloomy,
> I might almost say Spanish in character.

Unfortunately, Annan's plate did not capture for posterity the '2 ebonised cabinets from the room in the Winter Palace at St Petersberg in which the Emperor Paul was assassinated', which the Duke may have acquired during his visit to Russia. But the 1876 inventory makes clear, their drawers were

simply groaning with further treasures in the form of miniatures, prints from the Beckford collection, precious jewels and historical documents including '5 Lettres sur la Morte de Napoleon: Pauline'. In addition to books the library cases contained the 'Collar of Order of Thistle in drawer of Bookcase "O"', and on the extreme left of Annan's plate is a round table, surely the 'beautiful painted circular table of Sèvres porcelain presented by the Empress Eugénie to the Duchess of Hamilton née Princess of Baden'. A 'Mahogany library steps as chair' must have been a useful addition to these antique furnishings.

We can vicariously join a rather excruciating afternoon party in this room through the memoir of Professor Waagen, Director of the Royal Gallery of Pictures in Berlin, already quoted above, who had been sent to Britain on an artistic mission by the Prussian government, and published his observations on British collections in his *Treasures of Art in Great Britain* (1854). Hamilton Palace was 'the chief object' of his journey to Scotland in 1850 but his visit looked imperilled with the news that the Duke had had a riding accident, breaking his arm. In the end his visit went ahead, but it was coloured by the Duke being an invalid during his stay, and easily fatigued with an uncertain temper. This was offset for Waagen by the Duchess, 'a daughter of the late well-known Mr Beckford, a lady of the most refined and easy manners', whose conversation showed the 'highest cultivation of mind'; she herself showed him her father's Beckford Library.

Waagen thought the Palace a 'large and rambling edifice'. Thanks to Annan's photograph, we can imagine the party gathered around the centre table, while 'a bright fire was burning' within the porphyry mantelpiece.

> Here I enjoyed the favour of having the most
> costly Manuscripts shown to me by the Duke
> himself, the Duchess being also present and
> evincing a lively interest. My sensations,
> however, were of rather a mixed nature; for,
> much as I was alive to the honour of seeing
> these remarkable Manuscripts under such
> flattering circumstances, it was at the same

time not a little trying to be obliged to look through them in the most superficial way; for no sooner did I pause to consider some of the most beautiful miniatures more closely, than the Duke remarked that it would take weeks to study them at that rate, and urged me on. This being the case it was utterly impossible for me to make a single memorandum. I add, however, the slight reminiscences which I jotted down in my room in the short time before dinner . . .

Dinner was presumably served in the 'New Dining Room', also photographed by Annan, which opened from the library. Although the Duke had obtained a very lively design for this room in 1829 from Percier and Fontaine, with a segmental sideboard recess, the executed design was a more

sombre study in marbles, like a church in Rome, complete with the vast sanctuary-like recess for the sideboard, under a resplendently gilded Louis Revival ceiling. Presumably, at least the cornice was in *trompe l'oeil* marbling, a speciality of the Edinburgh decorator D.R. Hay, who may have painted these rooms. Rather perversely, given that the Duke's favourite black marble was the contemporary norm for dining rooms, here the Duke chose white statuary marble, possibly secondhand. The 1919 sale catalogue describes it as being carved 'with a basket and festoons of fruit, female busts and acanthus foliage', which sounds Palladian. The 1836 inventory reveals that this room was in process of being fitted out and the Duke was making do with mongrel sets of 'ancient' chairs.

The chimney-piece is described as 'A very fine

The Tenth Duke's new dining room, with its outstanding collection of paintings, was 'Louis' in inspiration with a rococo ceiling and curvaceous gilded chairs in crimson plush

Chimney of White Marble sculpted in the finest Stile', possibly one of the four chimney-pieces that the Duke purchased, according to Professor Tait, at the Wanstead Sale. The 'very handsome carpet' was 'new' and characteristically 'fits' with a fringe, unusually, around the skirting. The curtains were of 'crimson cloth', protected from the sun, as in the other state rooms, with 'green blinds Venetian'. The sideboards had 'very fine Slabs of Egyptian Granite on Slabs of White Marble' and the sideboard in the recess was so massive it was able to support, by the time of the 1876 inventory, the 'Magnificent Colossal Bronze casting of the Laocoon (from the Stowe Sale)' just visible in Annan's view behind the 'very fine Japan Screen with 12 leaves'. By this time the suite of Louis chairs designed for this room had appeared,

'36 chairs gilt legs Back and Seat covered in rich crimson velvet studded with gilt nails'; the 1919 sale catalogue says these 'nails' were 'metal-gilt Cherubs heads' borders. The telescopic dining table extended with nine leaves to 30 feet. Annan shows that this very long set was choreographed around the outer perimeter of the room with some difficulty. The gilt metal chimney clock, unusually, was English, by James Cox, the famous toy-maker who made the celebrated silver mechanical swan now in the Bowes Museum. The pictures were carefully hung to suit the available space, comprising the old Hamilton Palace Collection version of Van Dyck's equestrian portrait of Charles I, Pietro della Vecchia's *Four Fathers of the Church* and Van Dyck's *Duchess of Richmond with her Son as Cupid*. The other portraits in the dining room included *Philip IV of*

Spain by Velázquez and the remarkable portrait of Napoleon commissioned from David by the Duke in 1812. The *New Statistical Account* of 1846 states that there was probably £50,000 worth of plate, including a gold set, for use in this room.

The dining room, situated remarkably near the kitchen on the floor below, was supported by the adjacent ante-room with its 'Iron Hot Closets as fitted up & heated by Hot Water from furnaces in Cellar'. In the 'New Steward's Room under Mr Ramsay's charge', along with a mass of silk samples were the '6 pieces of marble paper intended for Ante Room'. The customs of the Late Georgian age were reflected in the 'Mahogany Pot Cupboard in shape of Pembroke Table', which must have been highly successful in disguising its true function as by 1876 it had been promoted to the dining room.

Balancing the library and the New Dining Room on the other side of the Duke's new north front, across the black marble stairs and with its enfilade landing supported by bronze Atlantes, cast by Soyer of Paris, were the 'Tapestry Rooms', or New State Rooms, so called to distinguish them from James Smith's late seventeenth century state apartment. In sheer scale alone this must have been the most ambitious modern state bedroom suite in any British country house of the period. These rooms were still being fitted up at the time of the 1836 inventory and their tapestries were stored in painted oak chests. The Glasgow University album includes a photograph of the fireplace wall of the outer room or drawing room, paralleled by a Hamilton Library Collection view of the opposite wall, also taking in the enfilade back along the stair landing to the dining room; it is exceptionally rare to have two views of a single room.

In March 1842 '10 Newly made pieces for Ditto [tapestry] for Panels over the Doors' were delivered to complete the cycle around the room. Each of the four rooms in the suite, the drawing room, bedroom, dressing room and boudoir, had modern 'Gobelin Tapestry Carpets' made to fit them, woven with 'Arms of France, fleur-de-lys, flowers and fruit in red borders' while that in the boudoir had a 'crowned initial L'. These rooms were deliberately intended to evoke Versailles, with modern ornamental detail in the curvaceous chimney-piece and lavishly gilded doors and doorcases in a flamboyant French rococo mode proportionate to the scale of the rooms. The chimney-shelf was low set at dado level with a broad shelf for the garniture – a feature just becoming fashionable in Britain at this time. This supported the 'superb chimney Clock Infant Satyrs playing on Musical Instruments, Dogs, Various Birds etc' and '2 Gilt Massive Candleabra'.

The principal piece of furniture in the room was the monumentally scaled 'exquisitely carved and Richly Gilt Large Sofa with 2 Conversation Ends and covered with the richest Gobelin Tapestry from Versailles', partnered by at least three sets of tapestry-covered chairs. In front of this stood the 'richly carved well Table lined with white satin and plate glass top', which looked and sounds like a vitrine but was oddly empty. At either end of the Versailles sofa were two Louis XVI secretaries, of which the one nearest the chimney-wall, 'with the centre panel a female bust with her finger to her lips representing Silence' by Oeben, subsequently went to the Rosbery Collection at Mentmore. Opposite the chimney-piece was a modern pietra dura cabinet, presumably by Hume, that was full of objets d'art from the Beckford Collection. Just visible on the extreme left is probably 'the Damascened Square chess table on a triangular column of Lapis Lazuli' with dolphin feet that the Duke of Milan had presented to a prince of the House of Savoy. The low four-fold fire-screens were an idiosyncratic feature of Hamilton Palace and there was another in the library. The curtains in this suite were of 'rich silk Brocade . . . lined Gold colour India taffeta & fringed and gymp'd complete'.

The effect of this suite owed everything to the sheer quality of these museum objects, which prefigured later plutocratic taste but with the difference that their flamboyant modern setting was unrestrained by dull academic notions of historicism. By the sombre dull historicism standard of the brown, crimson and black that prevailed through much of the Palace, these rooms were brilliantly cheerful, their colour set off by their white and gold panelling. Emptied of these treasures by the 1882

It was most unusual for Annan to have been permitted to photograph the Princess's bedroom with its tulipwood bed in green satin damask

LEFT: Princess's Marie's boudoir, hung with crimson satin damask, was the innermost room in her apartment and thus enjoyed an enfilade through her suite. Above the door is Swarbreck's painting of Mary Queen of Scots' bedroom at Holyroodhouse

sale, these rooms never again appealed to photographers and were to be the least recorded zone of the Palace.

If it was good fortune that Annan made this record before these art treasures were dispersed, what makes his record quite exceptional in the annals of early Scottish photography is his inclusion of the 'Princess's' rooms. For reasons of propriety, bedrooms, unless they had some ancient historical connection, were almost never photographed. These rooms must have been fitted up for the Duke's daughter-in-law, Princess Marie of Baden, when she married his son and heir in 1843. They were certainly on the second floor, probably immediately above the William Adam state rooms in the east wing. Although her husband, the Eleventh Duke died in 1863, Princess Marie was to live until 1888 and thus her rooms had little historical interest for the public; the Princess may have deliberately preserved them for sentimental reasons. They were barely affected by the 1882 sale as their contents were largely modern,

The dining room, denuded of the art collection by the 1882 sale, photographed in the early twentieth century by the Edinburgh Architectural Association; it still demonstrates meticulous standards of housekeeping with case covers on the chairs and a drugget protecting the carpet

although the Louis XV commode had disappeared in a later photograph, and the 1876 inventory is marked up in pencil 'None of these pictures to be sold'. The 1876 inventory does not make clear if Princess Marie moved to her mother-in-law's suite on the floor below when she and her husband succeeded as Duke and Duchess on the death of her father-in-law in 1852.

There are three views of this suite in the Glasgow Annan Album. The 1876 inventory makes clear that the enfilade view of the suite is taken from the innermost room, her boudoir, because hanging above the door was the Swarbreck oil painting of Mary Queen of Scots' Bedroom at Holyroodhouse, the most often depicted and photographed bedroom in Scotland and part of the Duke of Hamilton's Apartment at Holyroodhouse, a suite he held as the Hereditary Keeper of the Royal Palace. Thus the unusual view of the Princess's lace-draped dressing table must have been in her adjoining bedroom. Broadly these rooms retained their William Adam character with Clayton stuccowork, like the much grander Duchess's suite

below, but they had been made more ornamental with additional ceiling ornaments and new Louis Rococo Revival chimney-pieces.

Although the innermost rooms, like the boudoir, had crimson satin damask hangings, the 1876 inventory makes clear that the outer rooms reflected both the hierarchical fitting up and colour-coding of the Palace in that the ducal rooms were red, the Duchess's suite was in blue, although this could have dated back to the eighteenth century, and the Princess's bedroom was green. However there was also a sense of early 1840s colour harmonies because her sitting room's hangings were in 'amber satin' while the cloth on the centre table in the Princess's bedroom was 'A green cloth table cover embroidered in amber coloured silk', linking the tones of the two rooms together visually. The Princess's bed was 'a Tulip Wood Bedstead richly ornamented with gilt carving' with furniture of satin damask to match the 'green silk damask window curtains' with 'a richly carved cornice'. The chimney clock was by

'Mannheim of Paris cupids and a drummer on an oval plinth' with 2 gilt metal candlesticks and eggshell china vases.

Unlike the *grande luxe* of the public rooms of the Palace, these rooms have modern furniture and an up-to-date approach to notions of comfort although their silk hangings were unusually grand in a bedroom suite, presumably, like the gilding, in deference to the Princess's rank. The fitted carpet running throughout the suite is merely described as being of 'tapestry'; sadly its colour is not noted.

The cabinet in the Princess's sitting room was of modern 'buhl work' and the two couches were covered in amber damask to match the walls. The view of Lamlash Bay recalls the Duke's rebuilding of Brodick in 1844 for the newly married couple to the designs of James Gillespie Graham. This painting is now in the Duchess's rooms at Brodick, one of the few Hamilton houses to retain its collections intact because it passed into the care of The National Trust for Scotland in 1957. The chimney garniture comprised a clock by Deniere, candlesticks of 'Limoge enamel' and '2 eggshells mounted as ostriches with horseshoes in the beaks'. The most unexpected item in the sitting room was a poignant family souvenir: 'An occasional table of Mahogany on Turned Legs and Rails formed part of the furniture of Napoleon's Bedroom at Longwood St Helena'.

The 1882 sale of so many of Hamilton Palace's princely possessions, held discreetly in Messrs Christies' London Rooms far from the palace, caused a sensation in the art world. Their published catalogue is a substantial volume, with photographs that give occasional insights into otherwise unphotographed zones. The view, for instance, of the rock-crystal chandelier in the Hamilton Library also includes further details of the central bed of its ceiling. Perhaps the most evocative of these catalogue photographs is the view of the State Bed, described in 1876 as 'A carved and gilt Bedstead style of Louis XIV canopy covers of Gobelin tapestry lined with gold covered silk'. The Auctioneers more correctly identified the bed as 'Louis XVI', revealing a growing connoisseurship. The catalogue photograph seems to show it standing within a doorframe, but this may

have been an especially created tabernacle. It is shown with its unusual tapestry counterpane in Holland wraps, revealing the exceptionally high standards of house-keeping that prevailed at Hamilton Palace. By the time the bed passed to the Metropolitan Museum in New York it had lost its extravagant inner double

The Louis XVI State Bed as photographed for the 1882 sale catalogue, with the tapestry counterpane still enveloped in its specially tailored Holland case covers

Snapshot view of the rich plasterwork of the Tribune ceiling, by the Edinburgh Architectural Association c. 1920

lost their point and the sale was but the overture to a long and complicated unravelling, with the main line of the proud Hamiltons ending in a female heiress after the death of the Twelfth Duke in 1895. The coalfields that had fuelled this ostentatious display and the nineteenth-century industrialisation so besmirched the Palace surroundings that it was all but abandoned in the early twentieth century. It was used as a naval hospital during the First World War and afterwards the then Duke resolved to remain at the very much smaller Dungavel House rather than return to the vast and deeply unfashionable neo-classical palace. He instructed a second sale, this time with all the finality of approaching demolition. Scotland remains much in the debt of *Country Life*, whose photographer A.E. Henson travelled north to undertake the final deathbed photographic record in over 133 glass plates, many of which were published in my *Scottish Country Houses and Gardens: from the Archives of Country Life* (1997).

With nobody on hand to restrain them and the decision to hold the demolition sale already made, *Country Life*, who were famous for moving the furniture to improve the historical clarity of their photographs – 'It was worse than having burglars' was the comment of one house owner subjected to their method – indulged in an orgy of furniture removals to play up the earlier character of the James Smith Baroque South Front and the surviving historic rooms. The Hamilton Library Collection has an album with a complete set of prints made from the *Country Life* glass plates, including unique unpublished photographs taken from now-lost negatives of several four-poster beds including one in 'flowered pink silk brocade' known as the Duke of Newcastle's, named from the Tenth Duke's brother-in-law.

There is, however, one last collection of photographs whose casual, almost snapshot quality encapsulates a more genuine feel for the Palace at the end. Held by the Royal Incorporation of Architects in Scotland, whence the Amisfield and Balbardie photographs in this book are also drawn, their taker is unknown but for convenience they are called the Henry Kerr Collection, after the distinguished

valances and side-curtains of *trompe l'oeil* draperies, rendered in tapestry, surely nineteenth-century additions commissioned by the Duke.

The Hamilton Library Collections hold a number of photographs, including a set by Lafayette that reveal the triste atmosphere of the Palace after the sale. A particularly poignant photograph shows the Princess's bedroom stripped of its lace bed draperies but with a very ordinary high Scottish mahogany chest of drawers in place of the Louis XV tulip-wood commode that had matched the wood of the modern bed. The one rather startling innovation was the almost Art Nouveau Billiard Room, with a modish ingleneuk, although all in the Palace's prevailing dark oak.

Without their treasures the Palace rooms rather

antiquarian architect who may have brought some of them together and certainly used them for his 1933 article on the Palace in the *Transactions of the Edinburgh Architectural Society*. Only architects with a historical or technical interest could have been inspired to try to record the opulent plasterwork in the cupola of the Tribune – one of many zones of the Palace unvisited by the photographer retained by lofty *Country Life*. The Kerr photographs of the Gallery and New Dining Room catch a glimpse of the Palace's continuing thrall to the highest standard of housekeeping or more possibly its lack of inhabitants. The Edinburgh Architectural Association, from which the *RIAS* came into being, comprised the leading architects in Scotland but clearly there was no question of the vast Palace being undressed from its careful muffling in case covers for their visit, and possibly no longer the staff in residence to undertake the work. Thus both the Gallery and New Dining Room carpets are shown concealed by their protective 'linen' covers described in the inventories and considerable exertion would have been necessary to reveal the Gallery carpet, whose rectangular coffering reflected the Tenth Duke's new ceiling. Unusually, and an almost medieval wardrobe practice, the curtains have been removed to store with only the valances remaining, with their draperies tacked to their fixed curtain boards and protected by fabric covers.

Amid all this purposeful photography, it is a pleasure to come upon an inconsequential glass lantern slide, perhaps taken at the same time, that shows one of William Adam's broken-pedimented doorcases of the Duchess's Sitting Room, framing a great stucco shell by Clayton. It also captures the way in which the 'blue velvet pile carpet with fleur d'lys to cover the room', photographed by *Country Life* in 1919, was kept rolled up when the family were away, and just catches the corner of the still in situ pelmets in their white case covers from the, presumably stored, '2 sets rich blue silk damask curtains'. The chairs are the suite of Louis XVI-style oval-backed tapestry chairs, always in these rooms, and shown uncovered by *Country Life*. The gilt pier table, which may be a survivor of the late-eighteenth-century

fitting-out of these rooms, supports 'A wax statuette of William Eleventh Duke of Hamilton by Lewis under a glass shade' which was one of a pair with 'A do of William 12th Duke accompanied by a large dog'. But the atmosphere of the stripped-down room is melancholy and perhaps should make one grateful for *Country Life*'s attempt, as experienced house morticians, to dress the dead body of the Palace for a last lingering look. This sad corner of the Duchess's sitting room had once contained two of the Palace's greatest treasures, both now in the Metropolitan Museum of Art in New York. The superlative lacquer secretaire and commode bearing Marie Antoinette's monogram in ormolu, and festooned with gilded ormolu bouquets rendered with meticulous botanical precision, that caused the writer of the 1876 inventory to rise to a crescendo:

> A magnificent Secretaire signed Riesener 1790. And in all probability the suite of furniture as a whole is the most important and beautiful work of this kind produced in the age of Louis XVIth.

Snapshot view of a stucco pedimented Clayton doorcase in the Duchess's sitting room, with the curtains carefully in store, and the pelmets and oval chairs protected by their fitted case covers

CHAPTER FOUR

Douglas Castle

Lanarkshire

THE ANCIENT STRONGHOLD OF THE DOUGLASES, LEVELLED TO MEET 20TH-CENTURY IMPERATIVES

The apparently inevitable demise of the Adam brothers' atavistic Douglas Castle, at Douglas in Lanarkshire, on the eve of the Second World War, with no official agency in existence to make an adequate record of it, now seems a national tragedy. But there had always been a disparity, and sense of disappointment, in the gulf between the historic glamour attached to the illustrious Douglas family, woven in the very stuff of Scottish history from the time of Bruce onwards, and the unfinished fragment of the eighteenth-century Gothick sham-castle. This was perhaps exacerbated when Sir Walter Scott wove a romance around the original Douglas stronghold, 'Castle Dangerous', and thus he may deserve some share of blame for the later casual loss of one of the earliest and most ambitious Scottish attempts to recapture the spirit of antiquity. Douglas Castle is also a prime example of a house which disappeared on its demolition from the radar of Scottish architectural history and is now forgotten.

Its decline can be traced in a series of popular articles recording changing contemporary attitudes to this unusual building. They took their rather disparaging tone from the doyens of castle pundits, David MacGibbon and Thomas Ross, whose *Castellated and Domestic Architecture of Scotland* (1887–92) had been dismissive of the surviving portion of a round tower that was apparently all that had survived the great conflagration of 1758: 'Of the famous "Castle Dangerous", the fortress of the friends of Wallace and Bruce, not a trace now remains, the solitary tower which represents the old castle exhibits all the features of a structure not earlier than the seventeenth century.'

Gilbert Rae, writing in the *S.M.T. Magazine*, a continuation of *Scottish Country Life*, in December 1935, did not linger on the modern house but clearly felt much happier amid the dustier, and often fragmentary, antique tombs of St Bride's Church, where so many heroes of the House of Douglas lay. He gave no hint of the impending demolition and it was sheer good fortune that his prejudice against the modern Castle did not prevent him illustrating the noble mid-Georgian drawing room as well as the more modest Business Room, hung with portrait prints of the family.

LEFT: Late Victorian tourist photograph of Douglas Castle in its Georgian Gothick glory with carpet-bedded parterres, showing the new 1883 entrance hall and chapel on the right, alongside the ivy-clad stump of the only surviving tower of the old castle

ABOVE: Detail of the plasterwork of the dining-room ceiling

OPPOSITE: This handsome classical doorcase, apparently dated 1717, must have survived the 1758 fire but has obviously been reset and framed a humble joiner-made door

The castle's fate was announced in an illustrated article in the *Weekly Scotsman* on Saturday, 16 October 1937 bearing the headline 'FAMOUS SCOTTISH CASTLE ABOUT TO BE DEMOLISHED'. Written by the Reverend Thomas Hannan, this must in part have been a *rechauffé* of his earlier account of Douglas in *Famous Scottish Houses: The Lowlands* (1928), and like his book was illustrated with his own photographs, but now with a new topicality. Hannan had been writing about Scottish country houses since the end of the Edwardian period and he could not but be all too conscious of the changing times: 'It is the fate of many of the fine old mansions of the country in the present generation to be turned into hostels, educational institutions and other useful public establishments.'

But Hannan went on to explain that Douglas Castle had been subject to 'a different form of economic pressure':

> Its owner the Earl of Home has come to decision from a public and philanthropic need for the prosperity of the neighbourhood. New coal seams have been discovered and old seams

are being exhausted. The coal now discovered runs under the site and will undermine the building. It will also prevent unemployment.

This train of thought thus could not but spell the 'doom of a building not in itself very historical'. Hannan was a country-house buff who delighted in their individual characters, and now he took his readers on one last tour of this great house, with its odd entrance through a 'Hall of ordinary dimensions' leading to a corridor with the breakfast room and dining room opening off it on the left. The drawback of Hannan's descriptive approach is more than offset by the worth of his photographs. Douglas Castle had not proved particularly photogenic or easy to record, but his view of the rather austere dining room did capture, with a blind pulled down, the silhouette of the Georgian Gothick windows that were the dominant feature of the Castle internally; it must have felt a little like Leixlip Castle near Dublin in this respect. The dining room had full-length portraits in shapely Lely frames and an old-fashioned line-up of Victorian chairs around the perimeter. Unfortunately no prints of the Douglas Castle photographs have turned up among Hannan's papers except one of the very restricted entrance hall, and it is not possible to reproduce the poor-quality newspaper reproductions here.

Although a few stray nineteenth-century tourist photographs had found their way from family albums and the like into the National Monuments Record of Scotland, the only serious visual record of this very large house lies in the photographs retained by the family, along with the surviving architectural designs they commissioned. No formal record seems to have been undertaken on the eve of the demolition so it is simply a matter of good fortune that there are these few photographs as an all too inadequate souvenir.

The main published record of Douglas Castle is found in William Adam's *Vitruvius Scoticus*, of which the SNBR had acquired the Hon. Hew Dalrymple's copy in 1954. This published the complete design credited to 'Adam's Archts.' and it was thus one of the new plates infiltrated into William Adam's pagination by his eldest son, John. The opportunity

RIGHT: Detail of the
chapel and its interior
frieze in 1956, surrounded
by demolition

for such a radical new design is always said to have
arisen from the destruction of the earlier house in
the 1758 fire but the story is far from clear. This plate
shows that the executed part of the design was
merely the right-hand flank of an immense 'U'-
shaped design. The composition envisaged a Gothick
Castle on the grandest scale with a large entrance
hall flanked by a matched dining room and drawing
room on its left and right respectively. The hall led
through to a grand staircase lit from the court
enclosed by the 'U', and the stair in turn led to an
immense gallery 145 by 40 feet, presumably intended
for dynastic portraits like that at Holyroodhouse. This
façade was continued in circular closet towers, a
generous 18 feet in diameter internally, which rose to
an immense height of four storeys, above the already
vertiginous three storeys, not including the sunk basement of the main block. In the side flanks were long
chains of rooms, with corridors and anterooms lit
from the internal court, and beyond the main drawing
room was a private drawing room, taking advantage of
a bay in the centre of the side façade and leading to
the patron's private rooms with closets in the circular
corner towers. The family photographs include a detail
of a Baroque doorcase dated 1717, and thus a survivor
of the fire, which clearly looks as though it has been
reset. The architectural history of Douglas Castle
remains unresolved.

The patron was the First and last Duke of
Douglas, who is usually dismissed for the vapidity of
his ambition to build the largest house in Scotland, a
response underlined by his failure to realise more
than a fragment of the design. The sheer scale of his
enterprise must have been inspired by a serious
attempt to replace the burnt structure with something impressive enough to symbolise the historical
importance of the Douglases as the first family in the
country. The Gothick Castle was well suited to the
feudal character of his household. Its language was
borrowed from Roger Morris's pioneering Gothick
at Inveraray, built for the Duke of Argyll from 1744
by the Adam family. The Duke married in 1758 but
died without a direct heir in 1761, with only the
flank of his ambitious design built. The family's subsequent dramas were to be quite as sensational as

anything in their earlier history but the setting was
now the modern law-courts, where the succession
was disputed in the 'Douglas Cause' while the building works ground to a halt. The Duke had left
his estates to his kinsman the Duke of Hamilton, but
his sister had secretly married Col. John Stuart of
Grandtully in 1746 and given birth to twin boys in
Paris. The Duke refused to acknowledge the surviving boy as his heir and after his death the courts
initially supported the Hamilton claim, but the
House of Lords in 1767 reversed the decision in
favour of the nephew, Archibald Douglas.

When Thomas Pennant visited on his *Tour* in
1774 he described the castle as 'an imperfect pile'
but conceded that the 'apartments are fitting up with
great elegance' and felt that the new building, in
spite of its Gothick windows, showed that the
'storms of ambition' had been laid to be replaced
with a modern 'calm and contentment'. The family
papers include two photographs of the ceilings.
These are difficult to date but that of the drawing
room is certainly Adamesque in its geometry of
circles, but of quite outstanding flair in its
Gothicism. That in what was presumably intended as

the private drawing room is of a much more standard Adam repertory with rinceau scrolls and swags of husks but may been adapted to suit its temporary use as a dining room with its inner wreath of vines. The drawing-room ceiling was part of a suave overall décor, with an early Adam Ionic pillared chimney-piece, a handsome frieze and magnificent carved doorcases all contributing to merit Pennant's description of 'great elegance'.

The Duke's successors inevitably toyed with completing a design that was so obviously unfinished and plans survive from both James Playfair, in 1791, who proposed a central circular rotunda containing the staircase, and James Gillespie Graham, in 1826, whose grand design proposed editing away the Gothick windows in favour of something a bit more like triple arrow slits for a more archaeological effect. But nothing was done until the succession of the Twelfth Earl of Home, who inherited the Douglas Estates in 1877 from his mother, Lady Lucy Elizabeth Montagu, who had in turn inherited them through her mother, Jane Margaret Douglas, the eldest daughter of the last Lord Douglas.

The Homes, with their own seat at The Hirsel, were distinguished for their remarkable patronage of the arts, and it was presumably the Eleventh Earl, anxious to pay due homage to his wife's inheritance, who commissioned a magnificent table tomb in her memory from Boehm, the favourite funerary sculptor of Queen Victoria. In 1883, the Twelfth Lord Home, presumably more at ease with a now fashionably irregular castle than some of his predecessors, commissioned the architects Wardrop and Reid, of Edinburgh, to make a new entrance in a wing that had also to include a chapel. The entrance hall, as Hannan observed, was merely a flight of steps leading to the eighteenth-century corridor that served the Duke's public rooms, but the private chapel, at the hands of the London architect Henry Wilson, was to develop into one of the finest in Scotland as a result of his interest in metalwork and sculpture; Wilson subsequently became Master of the Art Workers' Guild. Happily, the Home family papers include a fine view of the chapel looking towards the altar that shows its exquisite early Florentine Renaissance-inspired polychrome decoration with remarkable tree-like trusses projecting from the bas-relief frieze to support the vault; there

ABOVE: The Arts and Crafts chapel, added to Douglas Castle in 1883 and fitted out by Henry Wilson, was one of the most richly decorated private chapels in Scotland

OPPOSITE: The chapel in its prime

LEFT: Detail of the painted barrel vault

The drawing room as photographed for *SMT Magazine* in 1935; it retained Owen Jones's decorations in tones of brown

is a perspective among the architect's papers in the RIBA Drawings Collection. Remarkably, the chapel alone briefly survived the destruction of the castle to have its detail photographically recorded for the SNBR by Kitty Cruft in 1956, surrounded by the shattered ruins of the castle's massive vaulted basement and a surviving round tower.

In 1872 the Eleventh Earl had commissioned a decorative scheme for the drawing room from the architect and celebrated interior designer Owen Jones. The result, in brown and gold, was intended to have an 'intermediate character between a Drawing Room and Library'. The black and white photograph of its ceiling in the family archives shows Jones's mastery of two-dimensional pattern in the intricate anthemion pattern, presumably realised in gilding,

within its central rose. Surprisingly perhaps, Jones recommended removing the swan-neck pediments crowning the doorcases, and after the demolition one of these shorn doorcases, stripped of Jones's graining, found its way into the collections of the Art Institute of Chicago. The family portraits from the Castle were taken for preservation at The Hirsel.

In an elegiac article entitled 'Douglas and the Douglases' in *The Scottish Field* in October 1965, George Crosbie felt that the town had been diminished through the loss of its castle:

The park is important. Not so much for what it has as for what it hasn't. It has space, three lochs, the Douglas Water, horned and hairy

Highland cattle, black cross-breeds, Ayrshires,

the fragment 'Castle Dangerous', ruined Army huts, a planned upland economy, and an air of spiritual desolation that makes it one of the perceptible vacuums in Scottish life and history.

Douglas Castle, the focal centre of its park and parish and countryside, isn't there. It was designed by Robert Adam for Archibald, first and last Duke of Douglas. It was doomed by the forces of war and state-change to which of course, the dangerous castle of the Douglases on this site had often before been subject.

In 1937 the Rankine coal-mine opened just beyond the park wall. Imperatives of its war-time operation evidently resulted, despite contractual precautions, in the undermining of Douglas Castle. The castle as a social-economic survival was at the same time under unprecedented pressures.

The mine closed in 1959, long before the bulldozers and earth-shifters finished off what was left of the demolition of Douglas Castle. They did so quite recently. Never has obliteration been more complete.

Detail showing the attenuated scrolling elegance of the Georgian Gothick plasterwork of the drawing-room ceiling, with additional two-dimensional painted ornaments by Owen Jones

CHAPTER FIVE

Panmure House

Angus

THE ROMANTIC JACOBITE SEAT OF THE MAULES, PLAYED UP BY DAVID BRYCE IN 1852, FAILS TO FIND A MODERN PURPOSE IN 1955

The demise in 1955 of Panmure, the historic seat of the Earls of Panmure just to the east of Dundee, was melancholy. Although the individual circumstances were unique, the factors that led to its demolition were common to many houses lost after the Second World War. The family had retrenched in the face of punitive taxation, and no alternative use could apparently be found for this great unwanted house. It is interesting to speculate whether Panmure might have survived had it not been so extravagantly inflated by Bryce's Baronial aggrandisement in 1852.

Unlike many other lost houses, the architectural history of Panmure had attracted antiquarian interest during the late nineteenth century. In 1879 Dr John Stuart had edited the *Registrum de Panmure*, an early eighteenth-century genealogical compilation by Horace Maule of Kellie, a younger son of the family who had held Panmure since 1224. Emblazoned with gold, and privately printed and distributed by the family in two resplendent scarlet-bound volumes, it could not but draw attention to Panmure's archives.

Because it was a new Carolean mansion, on a fresh site, and a putative early design by Sir William Bruce, Panmure was of great interest to antiquarians. The Bruce connection was soon refuted by recourse to the contemporary building papers at Panmure and credit properly assigned to John Mylne, of the dynasty of Master Masons to the Crown of Scotland. This conclusion was enshrined in the Reverend Robert Scott Mylne's monumental work of family history, *The Master Masons to the Crown of Scotland*, published in 1893 and dedicated to Queen Victoria. In 1666 George, Earl of Panmure had apparently decided to abandon the family's ancient castle and contracted with John Mylne to build a new house. On Mylne's death in 1667 work continued under the direction of Alexander Nisbet, an Edinburgh mason. The fitting-out was undertaken by James Bain, His Majesty's Wright, who contracted to plaster 'the withdrawing room in rich fruit work' and to copy the staircase from that at Donibristle. Earl George died in 1671 and his son and heir James completed the house, adding proto-Palladian wings to supply

LEFT: This High Victorian photograph of *c.* 1870 captures the suavity of Bryce's transformation of Panmure with a dramatic new central tower copied from Pinkie and ornamental detail from Heriot's Hospital

The forlorn entrance front of Panmure in 1953 shortly before its demolition

a kitchen and office court. Sir William Bruce is known to have designed the new gates with their handsome stone piers.

The house produced through this collaboration is best known in the engraved plans and elevation prepared for publication by William Adam in his *Vitruvius Scoticus*. These showed a modish double-pile house with a new sense of symmetry and regularity. There was a very large central room on the first floor, approached from the great stair, and advanced corner-closet towers on the principal front with ogee roofs that were to set a trend. As might be expected from such an experimental house, there was a marked awkwardness about the central feature, rather a rude attempt at a pediment. Professor Charles McKean has recently suggested that Mylne may have had to incorporate an existing structure.

This visual failing was soon to be more than offset by the Romantic Jacobite aura that clung to Panmure after Earl James joined the Earl of Mar's failed rebellion in 1715, was taken prisoner at Sheriffmuir and had his estates forfeited. The Earl is said to have locked the gates behind him against his triumphal return and they remained locked for ever, entering into legend.

The family fortunes revived in the nineteenth century and Fox Maule, named after Charles James Fox, who succeeded his father as Second Baron Panmure, commissioned David Bryce to improve the old house in 1852. By then the principal front of the house had been given a conventional Georgian pediment topped with vases to resolve the awkwardness of Mylne's façade. An elegant, economical proposal by Robert Adam in 1762 to reshape Panmure into a convincing imitation of a Palladian villa with corner towers had unfortunately come to nothing. Now Bryce reversed the orientation of the house and gave Panmure a powerful new drama by doubling up the corner towers and continuing the centrepiece of the main façade into a tower that soared above the new composition, taking its detailing from the tower at Pinkie. The side façades were given an extra projecting central turret, inspired by those at Heriot's Hospital, which was also to be the source of much of Panmure's new ornamental detailing.

The result transformed Mylne's rather ugly Carolean duckling into an elegant neo-Jacobean swan with a lively silhouette, in the process creating a much larger house that was well able to hold its own amidst its fellows. It may even have inspired a degree of local rivalry, since Bryce was invited to aggrandise both Kinnaird and later Cortachy on similar lines to Panmure. With its rugged masonry walls, it must still have felt very much like the old Jacobite Panmure that of course it still was, a tribute to Bryce's genius for this kind of sensitive transformation. Its site was a crucial element of its visual appeal; as Stuart said, 'to realise its grandeur it must be seen as it appears on the noble and commanding position which it occupies'.

Bain's rich fretwork ceiling survived within and Bryce had carefully preserved the character of the Carolean principal stair, which became the theatrical centrepiece of his new interiors. The new work was all in his characteristic boldly sculptural Jacobean manner with geometric panelling, rich fretwork ceilings and a great deal of heraldic devices featuring dragons, the family crest.

In 1860 Fox Maule also inherited the estates of his cousin Lord Dalhousie, the distinguished Governor General of India. The family may now have had something of an embarrassment of houses. His successors preferred their other Angus seat at Brechin Castle and when in 1902 the Fourteenth Earl married a daughter of the Earl of Ancaster, the new Countess employed Keeble to redecorate the main rooms at Brechin to display a suite of tapestries from Dalhousie. Panmure was relegated to a secondary seat. The romantic Jacobite shades, symbolised by the locked gates, thus descended on this sleeping great house, which was occasionally woken from its deep slumber by a shooting party, but essentially unlived in and preserved as a museum of family relics with a run of historic portraits and the state bed in which 'the first Pretender slept in the 1715 rising'.

The sudden death of the Fifteenth Earl of Dalhousie in 1950, at the relatively early age of forty-five, and unmarried, provoked a crisis for the family. The Earl, who had lived with his mother at Brechin Castle, was succeeded by his brother, the Hon. Simon Ramsay, who had been the MP for Angus. It was perhaps as a result of this Parliamentary experience that the new Earl sent a circular letter to all tenants on his Panmure Estates

Detail of Bryce's new fireplace in the entrance hall and his historicist plasterwork and panelling

on 3 February 1951, published in the local *Courier and Advertiser* on 5 February:

As you will doubtless understand, the question of meeting estate liability on my brother's death has caused me very great concern. I find myself forced to sell a considerable part of the estates that have belonged to my family for generations.

With the utmost reluctance I have decided to dispose of the greater part of Panmure, including your farm. I can only say how much sorrow this has caused me and my family.

In the midst of misfortune, however, there is one aspect which is consoling, I have been able to sell to trustees who assure me that it is their intention to hold the estate intact.

Photo by Colin McWillian in 1953 of James Bain's Carolean fretwork plaster ceiling of the Withdrawing Room

OPPOSITE: A dramatic view by Colin McWilliam in 1953 looking up the Carolean staircase reconstructed by Bryce. The dragons are the family's crest

This decision affected 52 farms, 23 smallholdings and a total of 11,070 acres. The newspaper published a map that graphically brought home the very large area of Angus that was affected.

The purchaser of the entire estate was the Harrison Trust, and Mr John Harrison, the head of this 'well-known shipping concern', reassured the newspaper reporters that the Trust had purchased the estate as an investment and intended to 'carry on'. Reassuring as this might have been, the Harrison Trust had now also taken on the unoccupied and now emptied Panmure House, after its historic relics had been transferred for safekeeping to Brechin Castle. They tried to find a suitable occupant but on 7 March 1955 the *Courier and Advertiser* reported that four years of effort to find a suitable use had failed: 'Apart from troops in the recent war, it has not been occupied since shooting parties made temporary stays early in the century. It has no electricity or central heating, and though it has 130 rooms there are only two bathrooms.' The paper went on to quote the Harrison Trust's factor, who pointed out that consideration had already been given to the house's demolition before their purchase of the estate:

Unoccupied for two generations the feeling was that if it could be used for any useful purpose it should not be demolished but strenuous efforts have not been successful in finding an occupier.

It was considered that the house could not be occupied by a private individual in these times, and an approach had been made to most of the national bodies and various commercial interests without success.

Such sentiments sealed the fate of many other unoccupied country houses at this time, although the historical summary of the house's history in these newspaper articles, which fully acknowledge the extent of Bryce's contribution, was unusual.

In order to demolish Panmure the Harrison Trustees contracted the services of Charles Brand of Dundee, the firm who had blown up Murthly so enthusiastically a few years earlier (see Chapter 16). The advert that Brand placed in the local press gives a flavour of a typical country-house demolition site during the 1950s:

OPPOSITE: The theatricality
of the vista through the
entrance hall to the
staircase is a characteristic
of Bryce's houses

FOR IMMEDIATE SALE:

The very fine oak panelling of the main hall; Oak Staircase; Windows; Window Panels; Doors; Door Panels; Oak and Pine Window Shutters; Shelvings; Skirtings; Miscellaneous Boardings; Mouldings; Facings; Flooring; Timber Battens, all sizes; Stone Pavement; Ornamental Stone Balustrades and Coping.

All Inquiries, Orders &C. direct to our site Agent, Mr Ralph Scott who is available daily 8 am to 4 pm Saturdays 8 – 12 noon.

Brand delighted in newspaper publicity and there was to be a run of photo-opportunities as blasting commenced.

The newspapers commemorated the loss in poetic prose, recalling the Jacobite connection:

DOWN COMES THE HOUSE THAT
NOBODY WANTS
NOW THEY'LL PLOUGH WHERE
HISTORY STOOD

[Panmure] will be erased from the landscape and its lovely site restored to agricultural use. Explosives will bring down the lofty towers and the fine stonework, which nobody wants, will be broken and scattered over the surrounding lawns, which will first be stripped of their topsoil by a bulldozer.

The stones are being taken over a mile to the great hole which was once Gallowhill quarry – the quarry from whence they were hewn.

There were, however, a few voices of regret. A *Courier* reporter was surprised to find that 'In spite of its age, the building and woodwork are in good condition' and was 'most impressed' by the 'exquisite moulded ceilings in the main rooms and halls'. The House already had found a role as a nascent tourist attraction, he reported, as 'each summer cars and pleasure coaches stop at the main entrance gates to allow passengers a glimpse of the imposing structure' and the empty house cast a spell over the surrounding landscape:

As I wandered through the vast policies of Panmure House on Saturday I was struck by the serenity of the place. You were in a world of your own where bird and animal life were unmolested. Even a pheasant was in no hurry to cross my path.

A 'GJ' of 'Dunfermline felt moved by these articles to write to the newspaper on 10 March 1955 in the hope that somebody might still do something to save Panmure, using arguments that were to gain force over the succeeding years:

I have never visited Panmure House but from the photographs and your reporter's description it would seem to have been well worth visiting. A mansion of such noble lines would seem to be worth preserving for its architecture alone far less its historical connections and it was therefore surprising to learn that approach had been made to most national bodies and commercial interests without success.

I know the National Trust is sadly handicapped with insufficient funds, but surely in order to preserve such a fine building it could have made some kind of appeal and I am sure it would not have failed in its efforts.

The Government should also help in saving such buildings from demolishers as it is the high rate of taxation which renders it impossible for private individuals to afford the high costs of upkeep.

We are proud of our traditions and while we wish to see new projects such as the Forth and Tay bridges, we must not forget our past.

But nothing was done and today we can only visit Panmure through the photographic record. Something of the timeless quality that hung over the estate comes through in the record photographs taken for the Scottish National Buildings Record in 1953, with the gardens no longer kept up, and the vast drawing rooms furnished with a random assortment of rough and ready chairs for a meeting of the tenants or a last dance. As always, Colin McWilliam's eye was drawn to the decorative and the quirky and

ABOVE: View of the great avenue, seen through the roofline strapwork, taken by Colin McWilliam in 1953

OPPOSITE: Colin McWilliam's photograph of the vista through the two drawing rooms shows them stripped of their finery, with a sorry line-up of ordinary chairs, but records the exceptionally fine Adam Revival Aesthetic wallpaper with its matching dado panels

he photographed the elegant Adamesque paper with its handsome Aesthetic dado in the drawing room, the view up the great stairs and the curly-tailed dragons crowning the strapwork high above the entrance front with the avenue leading away to an apparent infinity far below. But the unfurnished empty house, stripped of its romantic Jacobite accoutrements and portraits, and located amid these remote and silent policies, was understandably a daunting prospect to a potential occupier. The scale of the nineteenth-century work, in spite of its undoubted quality and sympathetic detailing, could not but dilute the few areas of authentic Carolean interior decor that had been spared in 1852. Even in 1976, when Alistair Rowan mounted his memorable exhibition celebrating Bryce's achievements, the tide of conventional taste had yet to turn in favour of the Baronial.

CHAPTER SIX

Brahan Castle

Ross and Cromarty

A HIGHLAND TREASURE HOUSE

Country Life traditionally turned to Scotland in holiday mood, and Lawrence Weaver's article on Brahan Castle, near Dingwall in Ross and Cromarty, was true to type in appearing on 19 August 1916 but has the melancholy interest today of describing one of the very few of these castles that has joined the ranks of lost, or more accurately ruined, houses. Even more unusually it came, according to Weaver, with a curse conferred by the Brahan Seer, 'whose cruel death at the hands of a Lady Seaforth brought continual disaster on the family'.

The rather too thorough modernisation of the early-seventeenth-century castle in the late eighteenth century at the hands of Lord Seaforth, a remarkable Highland patron of the arts, so diluted its Romantic potential and charms that its eventual loss may have seemed less grievous. Weaver's tepid enthusiasm for Brahan was shown in his decision to limit the only exterior photograph to half a page at the end of the article. At this stage *Country Life* had no staff photographer to despatch northwards and the Brahan photographs, by an unknown photographer, are adequate rather than elegiac. Weaver wrote regretfully, 'It has to be confessed that the castle owes the loss of its baronial features not so much to the perils of war as to the modernising zeal of the last Lord Seaforth. He removed its characteristic external features, but happily could not destroy the charm of the old rooms, and still less of their contents.' This view was endorsed by the Inverness Scientific Society and Field Club, visiting on 15 July 1922, who blamed the last Earl for 'dismantling' the Castle, and complained, 'The Castle externally fails to impress the visitor.'

The exterior photograph is positively forbidding, and at the scale it was originally published it was impossible to make out the fantastic rockery at the foot of the ivy-clad walls, an al fresco museum which included a cup-and-ring-marked stone, like Etruscan carvings built into a Tuscan palazzo, and the charming trelliage porch, so reminiscent of the American South. But this new rubble look must have been part of a recent renovation campaign, because earlier tourist photographs reveal a rather more classically sheer, even Italianate, look with a pale skim of limewash which threw up the engagingly lightweight

Country Life's 1916 record of Brahan's exterior; Lawrence Weaver found this photograph architecturally disappointing, but blown up it reveals the unusual trelliage porch, sheltering a display of horns and antlers, and the ancient carved stones displayed beneath the Castle walls

portico. A photograph in the Kodak books of Violet Brodie, now in the library at Brodie Castle, shows a house party enjoying its elevated and sheltered charms. The only clue to its Highland setting was given by two white-painted lead stags framing the porch; rather too reminiscent of Santa's reindeer, they had been removed long before the *Country Life* photographer called.

Weaver, by contrast, relished the interiors, especially the family's historic treasures, which comprised a sumptuous suite of tapestries, paintings, including a portrait of his heroine Mary Queen of Scots, and an exceptional late-eighteenth-century china cabinet with concave glazing, which must have excited the cupidity of the magazine's enthusiastic antique-collecting readership. The interest of these objects was enhanced by the Jacobite aura that clung to the Castle; the Clan chiefs of the Mackenzies, to whom Brahan belonged, were such staunch supporters of the 1715 rising that their stronghold at Eilan Donan Castle was demolished as a punishment, while General Wade, commander of the English army putting down the rebellion, established his headquarters at Brahan. As Weaver enthused, 'There are few houses about which the romance of the Highlands and of devotion to the Stewart cause linger more convincingly than Brahan, despite the way the fabric has suffered.'

Country Life must have appreciated the fact that in 1916 the family collections had recently been rearranged for optimum display, with the glory being the sumptuous Tapestry Room. It is difficult to think of any other room in Scotland which used tapestries in this spectacular floor-to-ceiling way with no architectural support, reminiscent of the mediaeval practice of humanising rough and ready castles in remote spots with hangings and carpets that travelled around with the family.

Weaver was inspired by this splendour to seek expert guidance concerning these tapestries from W.G. Thomson, and his information shows a new seriousness of scholarship which enabled him to date the suites to the second quarter of the eighteenth century from the signature of their weaver, 'V Leynier', and attribute them to Brussels

One of the tapestries retained a sumptuous Baroque border with almost life-sized animals

OPPOSITE: The Golden Bed of Brahan; the flat-woven carpet shows an art nouveau sensitivity

while relating them to other versions in different collections, including a set in Ghent; Weaver, writing in 1916, feared for 'how these had fared in German hands!' during the war. One of the panels depicting a scene from the life of Alexander the Great with a depiction of Darius's tent has a spectacular Baroque border with animals questing through fleshy arabesque foliage. Weaver wondered whether these had arrived to furnish the Castle after its spell as Wade's headquarters, but they are not mentioned in

the 1762 *Journal of the Right Reverend Robert Forbes*, published in 1923, which admired the paintings at the Castle, particularly the full-length Mytens *Mary Queen of Scots* in a 'frame of red fir', and noted that peaches and nectarines grew in the walled gardens while the house was very neglected. Another more exotic treasure, the 'Golden Bed of Brahan', said to have been brought to the Castle in 1618, was photographed but not published by *Country Life*, perhaps on account of the very modern decor of

the bedroom with its art nouveau carpet. This bed is now the centrepiece of Schomberg Scott's brilliant reconstruction of the King of Scots' Bedchamber at Falkland Palace, now in the care of The National Trust for Scotland.

Francis Humberston Mackenzie, created Lord Seaforth, Baron Mackenzie of Kintail in a revival of the title in 1797, began his career as an army officer but devoted his considerable abilities and energy to restoring the family fortunes. While Weaver deplored his drastic transformation of his inherited castle into a modern Georgian country seat, it is the sheer ambition of Seaforth's modernising zeal that fascinates the visitor today. Even the London architect John Plaw, in his *Rural Architecture*, published a design for Brahan with extensive office courts. Seaforth's aspirations are best symbolised by his 1786 commission of Benjamin West to paint the First Chief of the Seaforth Clan saving King Alexander III of Scotland from a stag, now the largest picture in the possession of the National Galleries of Scotland. Lord Seaforth created a modern parkland setting, incorporating North American trees, and is also celebrated for raising a new regiment of the Seaforth Highlanders in 1793.

Sadly the Earl of Seaforth's resources were not sufficient to sustain his ambitions and his later life was clouded by financial difficulties and sales of land. An early twenty-first-century assessment of Brahan, although dependent on this rather slight visual record, would surely view his contribution more sympathetically than *Country Life* did. Weaver himself could have told this different story as he had photographed (though he did not publish the result in *Country Life*) the very fine figurative chimney-piece with scantily clad maidens, standing on classical altars festooning Cupid with garlands of flowers, which seems from the epistolary record to be commissioned by Seaforth from the prolific sculptor John Bacon, favoured by George III, in 1796.

Brahan Castle was to be yet another Scottish country house whose loss was due to requisitioning in the Second World War, doubtless reviving memories of General Wade's residence. By 1966, when it was recorded in a perilous state by Geoffrey Hay for the National Monuments Record of Scotland, the office buildings had been converted to form a new house, while the Castle walls only stood to their full height on the east side and the interior had filled with rubble from the collapsed walls to the extent that 'A detailed analysis of the building would probably prove inconclusive owing to its ruinous and inaccessible condition.'

Geoffrey Hay felt he was just in time to record the surviving pediments with their star finials before they weathered away. This sad fate of Brahan is the more poignant when contrasted with George Mackie Watson's photogenic rebuilding of the Mackenzies' other seat, Eilean Donan Castle, for Major John MacRae-Gilstrap and his wife in the early twentieth century. Perhaps the Brahan Seer was to blame.

OPPOSITE: A previously unpublished 1916 photograph of this fine neo-classical chimney-piece, probably commissioned from John Bacon in 1796

CHAPTER SEVEN

Old House of Hedderwick

Angus

AN UNUSUAL ESSAY IN ALFRESCO BAROQUE STUCCOWORK

Of all the houses in this book, the Old House of Hedderwick, near Montrose in Angus, is the most haunting and perhaps the strangest. It has never been published but the survey photographs in the National Monuments Record of Scotland seem to catch the imagination of the people who come upon them. There is really no parallel in Scottish architecture for the resplendently Baroque and Berniniesque hovering figurative stucco sculpture of Old Father Time that gives a focus to this otherwise conventionally neat Early Georgian exercise in symmetry.

Hedderwick's modern conservation history began when David Walker, then a young civil servant engaged in drawing up the Historic Buildings List for the Parish of Montrose, came upon it. The excited surprise is still present in his voice today as he recalls, 'I simply could not believe what I was seeing'; there is a sense of straying into a lost domain, as in Alain-Fournier's *Le Grand Meaulnes*.

This Romantic reaction owed not a little to the Old House's decayed and tumbledown condition with a precarious fragment of roofline just holding sway over the encroaching vegetation, behind the eccentric obelisk-like central chimney. The photographs were taken in 1966, just in the nick of time because by the time of a later air survey in 1983 the remains of the roof had collapsed into what remained of the walls. It was too late for the Old House to be rescued and given new life, but it had the good fortune to be one of the first subjects to be recorded by the Royal Commission on the Ancient and Historical Monuments of Scotland after it had assumed responsibility for maintaining the National Monuments Record of Scotland in 1966. Although Colin McWilliam had sometimes made survey plans of complicated houses like Dreghorn on the eve of demolition, the Record had been chronically under-resourced. But now, under the wing of the RCAHMS, it enjoyed access to a staff of draughtsmen and photographers as well as academic investigators who since 1908 had been publishing outstanding county-by-county Inventories of those ancient monuments and historic buildings they deemed worthy of preservation. The Commission's then current publications on *Stirlingshire* (1963) and *Peebleshire* (1967) are surely among the most beautiful books on Scottish architecture ever produced on account of their survey draughtsmanship and photographic excellence.

In 1966 the Old House of Hedderwick was tottering into decay but the obelisk chimney still stood proud over the flying stucco relief of Old Father Time

Detail of the almost wingless and limbless torso of Old Father Time

The fast-disintegrating interior retained its shapel fire-surrounds

All these skills were now diverted to Old House of Hedderwick, which was also the subject of one of the first RCAHMS 'Record Sheets', which analysed the building in an orderly numbered sequence — a degree of sophistication impossible in the post-war shoe-string budget days of the Scottish National Buildings Record. Armed with this careful analysis alongside the photographs and the measured drawings, one can begin to understand how such an extraordinary building might have evolved.

The author of the Record Sheet was John G. Dunbar, the leading Scottish architectural historian of the day. It was clear to Dunbar that Hedderwick's Georgian symmetry, as so often in Scottish architectural history, was an attempt to modernise an existing intractable stone-built structure. A reused fireplace lintel in a nineteenth-century outshot at the back of the Old House was inscribed 'JS 1740 HB', presumably commemorating the marriage of one of the Scott family who had owned Hedderwick since the middle of the seventeenth century when the main block must have been built, and giving a convincing date for these alterations.

The mid-eighteenth century saw the zenith of Montrose's fortunes. Although today the town is bypassed by the main route to Aberdeen, at the time of Hedderwick's reinvention it was a successful port, drawing in skilled craftsmen to create a rich stock of grand houses of unusual architectural distinction.

Hedderwick's projecting wings, framing an appropriately Baroque forecourt, are presumably part of these same 1740s improvements, and it may be that the oddity and charm of the stucco solution owes not a little to an inability or an unwillingness to recast the existing structure. The second-storey windows of the main block which gave an air of grandeur were really a raising of the wall-head just sufficient to accommodate these windows, creating what is in effect a line of dormers. This kind of expediency suggests that money might have been tight.

Although much of the structure had collapsed into itself by 1966, the Record photographs show ambitious fielded pine panelling, incorporating an idiosyncratic rail-like narrow dado panel, in the first-floor rooms, which were finished with handsome moulded fireplaces with lively counter-curving sunk scrollwork panelled frames. The existing stairs leading to these refitted apartments, and possibly the old entrance door, were located off centre to the left of the principal façade, and their rather eccentric disposition was simply copied on the right-hand side to achieve a stab at the required modish symmetry. But there was not enough room on the left for the extra window required on first-floor level on the right, so the effect is bodged but still fools the eye. The projecting wings are of different widths and join at different angles, perhaps hinting at a more complex earlier history.

The unusual elaboration of the stucco ornamentation may be an attempt to provide visual distraction from these infelicities of symmetry. The elaboration of their egg and dart mouldings and doubled keystones is unusually decorative for Scotland, although the use of a lime-based harling was a commonplace protection for buildings in the harsh northern climate. Recently at Newhailes, built in about 1689 by James Smith, later the leading architect in Scotland, an original section of harled external wall was discovered behind Georgian extensions in a basement room. It showed how skilfully the builders had created, with incised lines, the effect of regular ashlar masonry, and Old House of Hedderwick had this same *trompe l'oeil* finish to give the effect of high-quality ashlar.

The chief visual distraction, of course, was Old Father Time, a familiar figure on clocks of the Early Georgian period but unusual as a bas relief. By 1966 he showed the passage of time rather too convincingly through the loss of both his stucco wings and other bits of his anatomy including his left leg, but enough survived to show his sculptor's ambition and attempt at musculature. The Commission's Record Sheet suggests that the arch-topped panel, then filled only with regularly jointed boards, that Old Father Time appears to bear aloft may have contained a heraldic achievement, though it is surely more likely that it was a sundial. Just enough of the ornamental acanthus border survived below the projecting panel to allow the Commission to reconstruct it in a measured drawing.

It is probably no coincidence that in 1740 one of the finest bravura displays of interior stucco was being executed at the neighbouring estate of House of Dun, now happily in the care of The National Trust for Scotland and thus readily accessible. The rebuilding of the House of Dun by David Erskine, Lord Dun, a Judge of the Court of Session, was a protracted affair involving several architects and must have been the leading architectural project in the area, setting new fashions and introducing Montrose to fresh aesthetic ideals. The house was eventually built in 1730 to the design of William Adam, with elaborations by the Jacobite Earl of Mar, exiled on the Continent. The resulting structure, with its Ionic triumphal arched façade and internal mezzanine creating an intricate nest of Chinese boxes, has a Continental flair reflecting Mar's familiarity with the latest architectural novelties in France and Italy.

The principal rooms at House of Dun were not fitted out until 1740, with Adam himself supplying their marble chimneypieces in 1741 and 1742. By this period, Adam had had the good fortune to attract the services of Joseph Enzer as his principal stuccoist and Enzer must have set off for House of Dun not long after he completed a cycle of work at Yester in 1739. The saloon at House of Dun is one of Enzer's most dazzling creations, with its almost full-size sculptural figures of Neptune riding the waves and Mars on a panoply of flags over its paired chimneypieces and scenes of hunting and fishing and a great panache of weaponry and banners in the coves above. Lord Dun's enthusiasm for this exuberant stucco display is also perhaps reflected in the small parlour where an earlier decision to panel the room was reversed and stucco was now applied, with no little complexity in the resulting wall planes. The doorcase between the saloon and the entrance vestibule has a similarly bold egg and dart surround, as well as the same doubled keystones as the window and door-surrounds at Old House of Hedderwick and very similar acanthus borders.

It is difficult not to think that the mania for decorative stucco at House of Dun rubbed off at neighbouring Hedderwick, and the latter's decorative architectural detailing, unusual for Scotland, could

easily have been created by a craftsman who had studied Enzer's method at House of Dun. Presumably the crisp egg and dart mouldings were cast in moulds, but their placement was worked out with care and a degree of precision, and the doubled keystones were chamfered to throw off the rain. But there were surely few people in Scotland, still less in Angus, who had the ability to mould a lifesize figure of Old Father Time with this degree of anatomical precision and sense of proportion, making it tempting to speculate that Enzer himself might have had a hand in his creation. By 1743, Enzer had returned to Yester, but on the 5 July William Adam wrote to the Marquess of Tweeddale to report that the stuccoist had died the previous week. Both the 1740s remodelling at Hedderwick and such later repairs as the blocking or reduction in size of some of the windows were carried out in locally made brick and it is possible that this experience of moulding bricks in Montrose might have encouraged the unusual choice of stucco for ornamenting the façade. It is the brick that gives the obelisk-like slenderness to the central chimneystack – although this could be a later repair or rebuilding.

The survival of so much of this Early Georgian work at the Old House of Hedderwick owed everything to its descent down the social scale during the nineteenth century. It passed first to the Robertson-Scotts of Benholm, but Alexander Warden's *Angus or Forfarshire the Land and People* (1884) says, 'The mansion is now occupied by several tenants of the labouring classes.' The infilling of the unused portions of the windows with brick probably reflects its conversion to a tenement.

In 1966 the Old House contained one last surprise: the second-floor stair lobby was decorated with panels surrounded by a geometric floral border. Because this decoration continued above an inserted ceiling thought to date from the 1740s alterations, this decoration may have belonged to the original building and thus be seventeenth century. The precision of the lining that surrounds the panels, however, suggests that it is probably an early-nineteenth-century copy of a fancy wallpaper from the time when cheap stencilled imitations were much in vogue.

The windows were given handsome stucco frames with bold egg and dart ornament more reminiscent of interior plasterwork

CHAPTER EIGHT

Seaton House

Aberdeen

AN ABERDONIAN PALLADIAN VILLA
WITH EXCEPTIONAL DECORATION

These photographs of Seaton made a deep impression when I came upon them by chance in the National Monuments Record of Scotland, and years later, when planning this book, I was determined to include them and find out more about this handsome but unusual house with its hauntingly beautiful interiors. Unfortunately I could not remember its name or where it was, so locating these prints required a week-long trawl through all the 9,920 photo-boxes, but the photographs, when I found them, more than lived up to my vivid recollections. Because its end in 1964 was particularly tragic it seems important to feature Seaton here in the hope that this house might find its proper place in the history of Scotland's architecture and decorative arts, and go some way to expiating its loss.

Seaton's location makes its loss particularly grievous in that it lay not in some out-of-the-way rural spot where few might enjoy its beauties, but almost in the shadow of the ancient St Machar's Cathedral in Aberdeen. With the visual support of King's College and the other buildings of Aberdeen University, the Chanonry of Old Aberdeen makes a convincing Scottish stab at mimicking an English cathedral close. As one passes the cathedral on one's left and crosses Tillypronie Road with its high stone walls, one enters, according to a signboard, and rather inconsequentially, 'Seaton Park', which plunges down to the swift-flowing River Don. Although the park is attractive enough with long-established trees, its *raison d'être* has disappeared with the loss of Seaton House, well able to hold its own in this first-rate architectural parade; now only the ghost of its avenues can be traced.

When the last laird, Major Malcolm Hay of Seaton, died in 1962 the Seaton papers were bequeathed to the neighbouring Special Collections Department of Aberdeen University Library in King's College. From these, and more particularly a heart-rending Obituary Notice of the House published by his daughter, Georgiana C. Williams, in the *Aberdeen University Review* (1967–8), some of the architectural questions can be answered but not enough to solve all the mysteries of this enigmatic and enchanting house. Georgiana Williams writes that she always sensed an air of melancholy that clung to 'a beautiful home but one which, somehow, even from my earliest recollection and through all the vicissitudes and turmoil of growing up with brothers, sisters, and an abundance of animals, pets of varied shape and size, still held

LEFT: Until the fire in 1963 Seaton House nestled under its hanging woods on the banks of the Don

View through the front door

re-hanging beds, including one with japanned cornices, recovering a card-table in green cloth, repairing and reupholstering furniture, including '10 french elbow chairs', and hanging new wallpapers, surrounding one of these with 'Olympian borders'.

The house the Forbes purchased so happily conformed with long-established Georgian notions of neatness, regularity and taste that it is difficult to date. Its principal peculiarity was the choice of building materials, as Georgiana Williams writes: 'Photographs of the house barely do it justice, for it was built entirely of small red brick, unusual in a granite district, with Aberdeen itself a famous granite city.' The design was clearly Palladian, but perhaps more specifically Gibbsian, with its stone window surrounds and quoining enlivening the expanses of brickwork; James Gibbs was himself an Aberdonian so this is not too fanciful a thought. A handsome detail characteristic of the architect, John Douglas, is the Venetian window with its circular head kicking up into the tympanum of the pediment and a stylish fluted keystone, balancing the fine pedimented doorcase flanked by tall narrow Venetian-like lights that support it. An Anglophile look with a villa feel is given by the tall ground-floor rooms, at a time when most Scottish houses had their principal rooms at first-floor level. This south front of Seaton looked directly across its park to St Machar's high on its ridge.

Seaton's broad expanse of glazing in the frontispiece, lighting up the staircase and contrasting with the plain neatness without, was its principal glory and as fine as anything one could hope to find anywhere in Scotland. By good fortune this was well recorded in the 1960 photographs, which can be studied in conjunction with Georgiana Williams' memoir:

an aura, an indefinable atmosphere that was somehow tinged with sadness'.

The Hays' part of the story began with the purchase of the existing Seaton House by James Forbes; a letter to him from Alexander Gerrard of The Strand, London, on 17 August 1782 ends with the 'PS I give you joy of your late purchase of the Seaton Estate'. James Forbes had married Margaret Gordon and their only child and heiress, Elizabeth, made a brilliant match in 1813 to a dashing military man, Lord James Hay, the second son of the Marquess of Tweeddale, who served in the Peninsular Wars, was an ADC to Wellington at the Battle of Waterloo and became Colonel of the 86th Regiment of Foot.

The family papers throw little light on the architectural history, but the photographs taken for Aberdeen Town Council Architects' Department in 1960 confirm that the Forbes were happy with Seaton as it stood and contented themselves with a fashionable redecoration. From 1787 to 1791, Alexander Scott, a cabinet-maker and upholsterer in Aberdeen, carried out various modest improvements including

> I can remember quite clearly my father talking one day to a very old retainer at Seaton. They stood in the hall, on the black and white stone-flagged floor of the great front hall entrance, that dominated the centre of the whole house. Portraits hung from the lofty height of the walls around, and a wide stairway swept down one side from a wooden gallery above. I stood by the heavy front door, which was open, its

iron-chain fastening hanging loosely to the side. The sun shone on the great brass knocker, and I remember how cool it was in the hall on that stone-flagged floor, though outside it was warm and the sun was shining.

By any contemporary standard this timber stair, with its spirally fluted double balusters on each step, would have been of the first quality, but what was exceptional was the splendour of its fictive painted decoration with imitation ashlar, festoons of fruit and flowers suspended by ribbons from shells, a Thornhillesque military trophy with crossed cannon and powder-flasks, the *trompe l'oeil* tabernacle frame and the fine simulated arched niche with its keystone. Similar painted ashlar has been found at Caroline Park in Edinburgh, thought to date from William Adam's improvements there in 1740, but the fine, if rather old-fashioned, and richly veined bolection marble chimney-surround gives this magnificence an earlier Baroque feel. This also tends to confirm Georgiana Williams' impression that this Palladian frontage, as so often in Scottish architectural history, was merely an updating of an existing house: 'The oldest parts were the north-west wing, where doorways and windows indicated the mid-seventeenth century residence.'

The grandeur of the painted hall was followed through in a richly rococo brass and glazed hall lantern recalling, with a degree of restraint, Chippendale's published design of 1762 for Dumfries House in gilt-wood, but the rather skittish plaster rose it hung from, with its whiplash thistle scrolls, looks more like an early nineteenth-century addition, when it was adapted to gas. Although this showpiece hallway would have made Seaton exceptional, it may have been its unpainted-over survival that was unique rather than its conception. Aberdeen is now thought of as a dour city, frowning on frivolity, but there is plenty of evidence to show that during the eighteenth century its citizenry were in thrall to all the latest fashions in decoration. As James Holloway has shown in his 1989 catalogue, *Patrons and Painters*, the Aberdonian artist William Mosman, during his studies in Rome, made a copy in

1736 of Guido Reni's *Aurora* in the Casino Rospigliosi for the ceiling of the saloon at Culter House, which had further decorative canvases by Mosman and plasterwork in the style of Enzer's work at Dun but was sadly lost in a fire in 1910. From the Montcoffer papers it is also clear that Duff was keen to create a Rococo drawing room in Aberdeen with Chinese papers and modish papier mâché ornaments.

But the sober splendour of this Baroque hall was challenged by a quite different spirit when Seaton was to be updated to reflect fashionable Picturesque notions, with the addition of louvred shutters to windows that were now dropped to the floor of the public rooms, and creepers trained across the brickwork: 'the house was covered with ivy, and how the leaves and tendrils of that tenacious foliage had to be trimmed back from the heavy wooden shutters that framed the outside of all the windows of the ground floor'. Although John Forbes lived on until 1838, Georgiana Williams implies that Lord and Lady James Hay lived at Seaton for most of their married lives. The sparse surviving vouchers show

The central Staircase Hall, with its painted Baroque rusticated architecture with niches, festoons of flowers, and a real carved timber balustrade and handsome flagged floor, was the glory of Seaton House

a certain activity with a flurry of new ironmongery in 1824–5 and gilding by James Hay in 1832 and 1841, graced with a pictorial bill-head depicting his premises.

These bills reveal the cosmopolitan much-travelled life of the Hays. During these travels they befriended a younger brother of the Orléans family, long before the succession of Louis-Philippe. This friendship had its commemoration at Seaton, Georgiana Williams recalled: 'I remember a large glass cabinet in the drawing-room, containing among other objects of art and interest two beautiful porcelain vases which, at that time I had not realized, were made to order for the King in a factory at Sèvres and presented by him to Lady James Hay and her daughters.'

The principal Picturesque feature of Seaton was its two conservatories at either end of the Early Georgian façade with brick piers matching the brick-work of the original house, as though Bernini had handed his design for the St Peter's piazzas to a firm of garden pergola builders. Presumably intended to support yet more creeperage, these may have had rather more character before their Picturesque latticed glazing was replaced with plate glass. These conservatories continued in wings with more of the matching lattice windows under balustrades, and one of the early photographs shows that the left arm was an open covered walkway. The Victorian photograph album also includes a portrait of Lord and Lady James Hay's daughter Georgiana, who remained unmarried, seated in one of these conservatories on a fancy bench, decorated overall with what can only be described as a parquetry of twigs.

This left conservatory opened from a newly added room and Georgiana Williams says this 'other' wing 'to the north-east, was early nineteenth century in date'. A side view shows a double range of French casements, protected by more louvred shutters, with a suspended balcony at first-floor level. The interior photograph of this ground-floor room presents a magical vision of the most up-to-date fashionable Regency elegance with its panoramic Chinese landscape wallpaper depicting birds darting between branches, framing an ogee

'Venetian' window. The central light was filled with glazed criss-cross trelliage doors that led out into the left conservatory, with the relatively narrow side lights panelled out to extend them in mirror plates and the whole surrounded by ravishing gilded tendrils of fruiting vines rising to elaborate pelmets topped by gilded flying cherubs, worthy in their fantasy of the Prince Regent's Royal Pavilion at Brighton. Who in Aberdeen at this date could have dreamt up this enchanting conceit? The brief slip of doorcase just visible to the left in the photograph shows modish architraves with corner blocks and distinctive doors of six equal matching panels, characteristic of the work of the Aberdeen neo-classical architect Archibald Simpson.

This spirit of architectural fantasy perhaps spilled over and infected the family's oral history:

Sometimes, when the river flowed high in its banks, you could see from the windows, through trees beyond, a gleam of water in the sunlight. There was a story, as stories there always are in places sufficiently antiquated to withstand them, that the river once overflowed its banks into the drawing-room to about half the height of its walls. Water-marks were certainly there to be traced beneath the delicate green of the wallpaper; even the gilded mirrors by the glass door that led out into the conserva-tory bore traces to verify the tale, but it was hardly credible, as the story no doubt became exaggerated in the telling, that Lord James Hay hooked a salmon in the drawing-room.

Without a plan, it is difficult to identify the other 1960 photographs showing decorative detail and fireplaces or work out their relationships. One of these, described as the 'East Front Room' and possibly Early Georgian, shows a dark-toned interior lavishly decorated with rich plasterwork under a modillion-bracketed cornice with scrollwork on the bed of the ceiling and a sumptuous frieze where a mask flanked by putti alternates with a different ornamental device with repetitive large flower heads pacing them out. Seemingly the same room had a sophisticated neo-classical fire-surround in fluted

Detail of stair with its
handsome Georgian
Rococo hanging lantern

white marble and windows with pelmet boxes by the same craftsmen who created the gilt ornament of the drawing-room windows. A further room, described as the library on the 1960 photograph, had a coved ceiling that had been marbleised with elaborate *trompe l'oeil* plasterwork, including a centrepiece with two cupids festooning a framed marble roundel with roses, of no little clumsy charm, while the walls had panels made up with wallpapered borders but framed in real picture-frame mouldings, presumably originally gilded.

A typescript catalogue of the books in this library, drawn up by J. Ogilvie Skene and dated 6 August 1959, survives in Aberdeen University alongside a cheaply duplicated catalogue for a 'Sale of Surplus Furnishings and Effects, the Property of Major J M Hay' to be held on the premises 'At Seaton House by Aberdeen and Northern Marts Ltd. Auctioneers on Tuesday the 29th September 1959'. The books, with their many histories of the Popes but brought up to date by Angus Wilson's *Anglo-Saxon Attitudes*, reflect the interests of Major Hay (1881–1962). Seriously wounded at the battle of Mons, during the First World War, he was captured by the Germans but returned 'to save the cost of the funeral'; he recovered to pursue his literary interests as a member of a Catholic family who believed that Protestant historians had allowed their prejudices to colour their judgement, and developed a lifelong interest in the Zionist cause. The sale catalogue of the 'Surplus Furniture' is too telegraphic to be anything other than tantalising, with its 'antique table on cabriole legs', '6 mahogany hall chairs' and '2 antique circle marble top hall tables with cabriole

legs', brought up to date with a 'walnut cocktail cabinet'.

After the Hays had left Seaton the end was brutal, as Georgiana Williams relates:

> In years to follow, the younger generation of Hays dispersed and went their separate ways. The house and grounds became public property, but though the grounds were soon transformed into a park with lovely walks beneath shady trees along the river bank, the house stood in empty isolation until such time as it could be decided what was to become of it, how in the interest of the public to make use of it, and yet preserve in its essence the old-world charm and dignity of its structure, the historical and sentimental interest of the house that dominated the landscape around.
>
> Nothing had as yet been decided when, one evening in the late spring of 1964, when rhododendron bushes by the front of the house were ready with the first gleam of sunshine to burst into a colourful mass of scarlet and palest pink, when bluebells on the bank by the dining-room windows spread a carpet of blue in the long, lush grass, and trees in their fresh green glory cast shadows over the soft, new grass where rabbits always abound, vandals appeared upon the scene and set the house on fire.
>
> It took several days for the smouldering remains to become completely extinguished and for the ashes to grow cold. Some of the structure, which managed to withstand the ravage of fire, stood starkly upright, as if in ghostly protest at the incomprehensible power and capability of Man for destruction.

The account in the *Scotsman* on 24 May 1963, headed 'Fire Destroys Fine Old Aberdeenshire House', records that the Hays had departed in 1956 and 'Aberdeen Corporation acquired the house and part of the estate, and a committee were considering turning part of the house into a regional museum'. How little could Aberdeen afford to lose, with such apparent carelessness, this precious and sparkling Georgian jewel.

CHAPTER NINE

Amisfield

East Lothian

ONE OF THE EARLIEST PALLADIAN VILLAS IN SCOTLAND

Crucially important in the history of Scottish architecture, Amisfield represents a daring act of patronage that was to result in Scotland's first orthodox Palladian country house. Its begetter was Francis Charteris, the second son of the Fifth Earl of Wemyss, who was educated at Eton and then travelled abroad, an experience that must have developed his aesthetic awareness. His family fell under a cloud when his elder brother, Lord Elcho, espoused the cause of Bonnie Prince Charlie; after the defeat at Culloden in 1746 he fled abroad, his right to inherit the title forfeited. Francis succeeded to his mother's estates, which included Amisfield near Haddington in East Lothian, and commissioned the new house in 1756, the year of his father's death.

It was a time when most Scottish landowners were happy enough to rely on native talent, but Francis sought out the English architect Isaac Ware, whose reputation had been established through masterpieces like his Chesterfield House in Mayfair and was consolidated in his canonical publication *The Complete Body of Architecture* (1756), which includes plates of the plan and principal elevation of Amisfield. The result was a house with a handsome Ionic portico that would not look out of place in the Thames Valley. The photographs here reveal that it was not realised in precise conformity with Ware's published designs, as his plan does not show the lateral canted bays. That an executed design should depart from the published intention is not particularly unusual, but it is at least as likely that the design of Amisfield continued to evolve during the patron's lifetime.

Francis Charteris was to develop into the greatest patron of architects in eighteenth-century Scotland, constantly testing new talent and always in search of fresh ideas. His enthusiastic patronage was to leave his estates so well furnished with country houses in various states of completion that he may perhaps be held, at least indirectly, responsible for the rationalisation that was to lead to the demolition of Amisfield in 1925. In 1784 Francis commissioned some alterations to Amisfield from John Henderson, a fresh young Scottish architect who was to be tragically short-lived. Henderson had completed his architectural education in Rome and has attracted the attention of later historians as a result of his quarrel with the young John Soane, while they were both in Italy, over the patronage of the Earl-Bishop of Derry. Henderson died early in 1786 and it is unlikely that his

LEFT: The North Front of Amisfield, viewed from the River Tyne

The South Front

planned alterations were ever completed, but he did give the House a fashionably updated neo-classical look by concealing Ware's pitched roofs behind a high balustrade, creating a flattened silhouette. This new verticality was also increased by the new sweep of curving ramps, bringing carriages up to the arcade below the portico.

Unfortunately, the photographic record gives little indication of how Henderson's new wings looked because the photographer concentrated on the central Ware block. The one interior photograph of the dining room shows how Ware's high coved, and presumably panelled, Palladian rooms were neo-classicised with a deep but lightly modelled frieze of vases with floral garlands that is very like the deep friezes executed by Nisbet, the Edinburgh plasterer and later architect, in Henderson's new Assembly Rooms in Edinburgh's George Street, which also remained unfinished on his death. The light timber or plaster strips, decorated with husks that pace out the

niches, look like vestigial panelling and one niche retains a classicising statue; both Henderson and his patron were to be leading supporters of Mrs Coade's imitation stone manufactory and imported her productions freely into Scotland. Henderson may also be responsible for the chastely neo-classical walled garden, which has survived the demolition of the house, with its elegant porticoed round temples set across each internal corner. Another of the garden buildings has a markedly chinoiserie-rococo character, demonstrating his patron's confident freedom of choice in selecting from the architectural styles that fashion dictated at a particular moment.

If the original Palladian interiors of Amisfield were ever completed to Ware's designs, it is clear that, as at Chesterfield House, the orthodoxy gave way to a more frivolous rococo character, as proved by the two celebrated canopied chinoiserie daybeds. Designed to mimic miniature garden buildings, these striking pieces of furniture are known to have

originated at Amisfield and are still in family possession. They have traditionally been attributed to Chippendale because, very unusually, both Francis Charteris and his wife Catherine, a daughter of the Duke of Gordon, were subscribers to his *The Gentleman and Cabinet-Maker's Director* (1754). These daybeds, the subject of a *Country Life* article by Christopher Hussey in 1965, inspired archival research into the origins of Amisfield which revealed that John Baxter may have been the Scottish contractor who built the house but threw no light on the maker of the daybeds themselves. The glory of Amisfield, however, was its outstanding collection of Old Masters, and Francis supplied a catalogue of these 'capital paintings' to Volume I of *Archaeologia Scotica* in 1792.

But in 1784 his attention had strayed from Amisfield with the purchase of the Gosford estate on the shores of the Firth of Forth, which he had come to know through his love of golf, which he played

on the Links there. He proceeded to improve the existing house while, at the same time, commissioning Robert Adam to design a grand new house, specifically adapted with a suite of large well-lit rooms for the art collection. He soon made Amisfield over to his son. After his brother's death in 1787 Francis became known as Lord Wemyss, though the title remained technically in abeyance. When he died in 1808 he was laid to rest in his last great architectural project at Gosford, a pyramidal mausoleum whose designer is unknown. With two houses to choose from on the Gosford estate, his descendants vacillated between the two until 1883, when the then Earl of Wemyss employed his architectural protégé William Young to complete the Adam design with appropriate additional modern conveniences, including a vast pillared alabaster hall that anticipates the splendour of Young's executed designs for Glasgow City Chambers. The old house at Gosford was then demolished. It may have been on account of

South-west view of Amisfield with temporary wooden fence enclosing the demolition site in 1925, showing the bay windows of the side façade and the longer side windows on the attic storey

these renewed building works at Gosford that John Small's *Castles and Mansions of the Lothians* stated in 1883 that several of the works of art at Amisfield had been transferred 'in recent times' to Gosford. But Small also provides a fascinating detail about Amisfield that his black and white photograph could not convey, stating that this Palladian house had been built of 'red coloured sandstone'. This can be readily proved; in the 1920s materials were valued and carefully recycled in modern buildings, and Amisfield's stones were incorporated in the Golf Club House at Longniddry. The statuary along Henderson's roofline was also rescued at that time.

The record of Amisfield's demolition in 1925 is almost as significant as the design of the house itself. The five photographs reproduced here form a composite set. One – the standard bucolic picturesque view with the portico seen from across the River Tyne – must have been an existing commercial tourist photograph intended for albums and postcards, and contrasts with the four others, which have the rawness of a demolition site. It is interesting that both types of photograph were felt necessary for a record. The final photograph features the rough picket fence enclosing the demolition site, broken windows, and the isolated castellated tower still standing amid rubble, while in the exceptionally rare interior view the architraves have already been torn from the doorway. These photographs build up a complete three-dimensional sense of Amisfield, and point up anomalies like the larger attic windows of the right-hand side elevation, which suggests the presence of a typical Scottish skied attic library as survives at both Arniston and Duff House.

The photographs of Amisfield reproduced here survive in the Library of the Royal Incorporation of Architects in Scotland, along with a letter from W. Glassford Walker to Stuart Kaye, the Secretary of the Edinburgh Architectural Association, which states:

> I send herewith 5 photographs of Amisfield House, Haddington, which was recently demolished. These have been sent this week by Mr George Sinclair, architect, Haddington, to

OPPOSITE: The dining room at Amisfield during demolition in 1925, with the door facings already removed but a classical statue still *in situ*

be kept as a record of the building. He says that he has plans of the House should you wish to refer to them.

This deliberate last-minute attempt to capture the quality and character of this exceptional house for posterity reflects a new consciousness that demolition of such an important Scottish building was not just a private matter for the noble family concerned. Not only that; it shows an emphasis on record-keeping that was an important step in the development of the record photography that later became the norm in the Scottish National Buildings Record.

LEFT: North-east view of Amisfield during demolition, showing Henderson's curving carriage ramps to the principal door

CHAPTER TEN

Gordon Castle

Morayshire

ONCE ONE OF THE GREATEST HOUSES
IN THE NORTH OF SCOTLAND

Although Gordon Castle cannot quite claim to be a lost house, in that substantial parts happily survive, enough has gone to be regretted because the ducal palace of the Gordon dynasty was one of the great houses of the north of Scotland, where great houses are thin on the ground. Its end is poorly documented but the final before and after photographs graphically illustrate the drastic pruning that was to be its fate but also ensured its survival.

Much of its charm depended on the rather half-hearted classicising symmetry that was imposed on the ancient tower house during the eighteenth century by the Second and Fourth Dukes of Gordon, who wished to shine as patrons of contemporary art while demonstrating their pride in their long family history. At first glance, it might look like rather an absurd pasteboard fort run up cheaply on the grandest scale – it was 568 feet long – with little architectural merit, but much of the ancient structure survived internally, giving a quirkiness to its interior spaces that successive Dukes were apparently happy to tolerate.

Gordon Castle's great height and bulk reflected its origin in the magnificent ancient tower-house of Bog-of-Gight, already perceived as a palace, with a lively decorative skyline silhouette similar to that of the ruined Huntly Castle, another of the Gordons' strongholds. Eighteenth-century survey drawings and plans show how much of this tower-house was regularised away. The first wave of improvement was carried out by Alexander, Second Duke of Gordon in the 1720s and reflected his cosmopolitan interests, as James Holloway has shown in his Scottish National Portrait Gallery exhibition catalogue *Patrons and Painters: Art in Scotland 1650–1760* (1989). The Gordons were one of the leading Catholic families in Scotland and the Duke espoused the Jacobite cause in 1715 but returned home, surrendered and was pardoned, with his estates restored, after a spell in prison.

Before his succession to the title, Duke Alexander had travelled in Italy and struck up a friendship with Cosimo III, Duke of Tuscany, after whom he named his eldest son. During a later visit to Rome in 1717, the Duke met the Aberdonian artist John Alexander, who had several Jacobite patrons, including the exiled Earl of Mar. This contact led to what James Holloway has described as 'one of the most important decorative projects in Scotland in the eighteenth century', when the

LEFT: 19th-century tourist view of the Garden Front of Gordon Castle, with the central ancient tower screened by picturesque foliage

The entrance front
of Gordon Castle with
demolition under way

Duke commissioned Alexander to paint the ceiling of the principal staircase at Gordon Castle. Alexander's sketch proposal, dated 1720 and now in the National Gallery of Scotland, depicts the Rape of Prosperine in a *trompe l'oeil* plasterwork frame and derives from a ceiling designed by his master, Chiari, for the Palazzo Barberini. It was executed in 1725, after Alexander's return to Scotland, and the bill survives for 'a large history painting, cloth &c', but alas there seems to be no surviving photograph of it. The Duke's Italian experiences may have also inspired the sculpture collections at Gordon Castle, beginning with Foggini's bust of Duke Cosimo for which John Alexander designed a pedestal; he also produced designs for vases to decorate the gates.

Another Alexander, the Fourth Duke of Gordon was to continue his grandfather's zeal for improvement after he married Jane, the daughter of Sir William Maxwell of Monreith, and famed for her beauty, in 1767. After the Peace of Paris in 1763 the Duke had travelled abroad and it was presumably

then, in Italy, that he began to order further classical statuary for Gordon Castle. These purchases, which included marble copies of the Apollo Belvedere and the Venus de Medici, gave a distinctive neo-classical character to the Castle's interior. The Duke wanted to classicise the exterior to match, and commissioned designs from John Adam in 1764 and an architect of Huguenot extraction, Abraham Roumieu, whose plans show the great complexity and scale of the existing ancient building. In the end this commission went to the young John Baxter in 1769, who inherited the ducal patronage on the death of his father, a builder, who had carried out commissions for the Gordon clan including the building of Haddo House. Like so many second-generation eighteenth-century architects, including the Adams and the Mylnes, his father sent him to Rome to complete his studies, enabling the young Baxter to make the leap to architect status.

The modernisation of Gordon Castle tested the young architect's newly acquired skills because

Gordon Castle before and after the demolition of the central block; the ancient tower alone remained

the Fourth Duke insisted on preserving the tall and slender old tower as the centrepiece of the South or Garden Front – which, at a stroke, skewed any hope of conventional classical symmetry. As Ann Simpson demonstrated in *The Bulletin of the Scottish Georgian Society*, no. 2 (1973), Baxter's solution was ingenious: he created a platform at *piano nobile* level that gave an apparent symmetry. He continued this façade out into wings, with linking corridors, avoiding monotony through the introduction of unexpectedly lively projecting corner bays and the choice of circular-headed windows on the piano nobile. The whole vast design was tightly knitted together by Baxter's machicolations, which harmonised the new with the old work, and the castellated parapet on the platform continued as a belt to break up the unusual height of the inevitably rather gloomier north or entrance façade. Such was Baxter's skilful manipulation of the Old Castle that it cannot have been immediately apparent that the three bays that lit the existing dining room on the *piano nobile*, to the left of the projecting ancient tower, were only answered by two bays of the new billiard room. Baxter's plan shows a mass of intractable ancient masonry in this zone of the Castle, which may explain why the east pavilion also had to contain the private rooms of the Duchess and the nurseries over the kitchen offices.

Built in white Elgin freestone, this rather forbidding exterior gave no hint of the dazzling neo-classical palace that lay within. Baxter's designs for the interiors of Gordon Castle must be amongst the most beautiful architectural drawings for any country house in Scotland. Although their plaster ceilings were Adamesque, Baxter's brilliant draughtsmanship gave them an unusual vivacity and flair. Work began in 1771 with the casing-up of the statues of Apollo Belvedere and Venus in the Old Dining Room in preparation for their removal to new positions in Baxter's redecorated hall, where they joined busts of Homer, Caracalla and Marcus Aurelius. The plasterer was Philip Robertson, who interpreted Baxter's ornamental designs, and the new rooms were painted by the house-painter Walter Smeiton, whose bills, as Ann Simpson shows, give

unusually full details of their colour schemes. The hall, with its new statuary groupings, was decorated in straw colour on both the ceiling and walls; the newly redecorated dining room had a white ceiling picked out in grey with French grey on the walls, while its new screen of columns at the service end were of scagliola; and the drawing room had a ceiling picked out in different colours, papered walls and the window linings picked out in silver grey against white.

Baxter's arrangements at the Castle were to prevail unaltered to the end, although the Aberdeen architect Archibald Simpson was employed by the Fifth Duke to rebuild the east wing after it was almost totally destroyed by fire on 11 July 1827. Neale's *Views of the Seat of the Noblemen and Gentlemen in England and Wales, Scotland and Ireland* (1823) gives a good impression of the Castle's interiors:

The hall is embellished by a copy of the Apollo Belvidere, and of the Venus de Medicis, beautifully executed of statuary marble by Harwood. Here also, by the same ingenious statuary, are busts of Homer, Caracalla, M. Aurelius, Faustina and a Vestal. At the bottom of the great staircase are busts of Julius Caesar, Cicero, and Seneca, on marble pedestals. With these last stands a bust of Cosmo the Third, Duke of Tuscany – connected with the family of Gordon.

The first floor contains the dining-room, and several other elegant apartments. The sideboard is within the recess of the dining-room, separated by lofty Corinthian columns of Scagliola, in imitation of verd-antique marble. In this room are copies by Angelica Kauffman of Venus and Adonis, and of Danae, by Titian; of

Late 19th-century view of the entrance hall with a stone pavement and grained ceiling beams

OPPOSITE ABOVE: Detail of Philip Robertson's plaster coat of arms just clinging to the laths of the entrance hall, 1952

OPPOSITE BELOW: Detail of Baxter's elegant plasterwork in the soffit of one of the circular-headed windows, 1962

Thomas Hannan's 1920s
photograph of the entrance
hall shows the ceiling
painted white and the
stone slabs softened with
tartan carpet

Abraham and Hagar, of Joseph and Potiphar's wife by Guercino; of Dido and St Cecilia, by Domenichino; besides several portraits. In the drawing-room is a portrait of the Duke of Gordon, by Raeburn; and of the Duchess, by Sir J Reynolds; and some beautiful screens executed by the ladies. In the breakfast room is a copy, by A. Kauffman, of the celebrated St Peter and St Paul, the masterpiece of Guido Rheni, esteemed the most valuable in the Lampiori palace, at Bologna, and one of the best paintings in the world.

The Library is in the third, and the music room in the fourth floor, both directly over the dining-room and of the same dimensions.

These arrangements still prevailed in the description published in *Morayshire Described* (1868) but there was now a small theatre as well as the library on the third storey.

The long survival of this decoration may have owed something to the complications that followed the death of the Fifth Duke. In 1813 he had married Elizabeth Brodie, but they were childless and the Duchess devoted her long widowhood to good works. When she died the entire contents of her dower house, Huntly Lodge, were sent to enrich Brodie Castle with portraits, French furniture, superb porcelain and, confusingly, a second version of the Venus de Medici. The Dukedom became extinct until it was revived in 1879 for the Duke of Richmond, who was a descendant of the last Duke's sister, Charlotte, who had married the Duke of Richmond in 1789.

After the Second World War Gordon Castle was in a very sorry state. The furniture had been dispersed by auction in 1938. A note in the introduction to the catalogue of the Gordon Muniments, now in the Scottish Record Office, says that Gordon Castle was requisitioned by the War Department, with the Duke retaining control only of the muniment room and the wine cellar; the troops quartered at the Castle were unruly and disturbed the papers, which had to be transferred to Edinburgh for safety in 1947.

Gordon Castle was one of the first country houses to be visited by the young Kitty Cruft, before she joined the Scottish National Buildings Record, when she accompanied her father on a visit to see if it was suitable for use by the mutual holiday company for which her father worked. She recalls that the bathrooms, which were stacked on top of each other to the full height of this immensely tall house, were thick with the red dust from the well-entrenched dry rot. In 1952 the Ministry of Works made a photographic record of the exterior but there now seems to be no record of their advice, which required the salvation of the original tower by pruning away of the dry-rot-infested Castle. The wings survived, with one being converted to provide an independent house, retaining much of Simpson's decorative interior work, while the other became a steading.

The archival record of Baxter's improvements in the Gordon Papers is so thorough that it is frustrating that there is no photographic record of these fine neo-classical interiors, particularly Robertson's plasterwork – presumably because of the intense grip that the dry rot had taken – and thus there is even some uncertainty as to how long Alexander's staircase ceiling had survived. In 1952 the Ministry of Works photographers took a photograph of one of Robertson's armorial trophies with the deerhound supporters of the ducal arms in the entrance hall, which was happily rescued and installed in the new house excavated from the wing. In 1962 Alistair Rowan photographed a surviving fragment of

plasterwork on the soffit of one of the arched window bays. Then a tourist photograph of a trophy of arms and standards in the entrance hall flanked by the Apollo and Venus on their sumptuous coloured marble bases, with sculpted dies, turned up in the records of British Rail when these passed to the National Archives of Scotland.

But these could only tantalise, and thus it was a great thrill when during the preparation of this book I recognised three more interiors of the Castle among the papers of the Rev. Thomas Hannan, which were presented by his family to the National Monuments Record of Scotland in 1997. Today Hannan is remembered for his book *Famous Scottish Houses: The Lowlands* (1928), which brought together the articles he had produced and illustrated over many years. His papers reveal that his vocation lay in home missionary work in the diocese of Edinburgh and he lived in Musselburgh. In 1911, he wrote to Lawrence Weaver, the architectural editor of *Country Life*, offering him articles on Winton, Pinkie and Newhailes; in the event the Winton article appeared in 1912 under Weaver's name. The width of Hannan's interests may have caused the downfall of his relationship with the very architecturally focused Weaver; he was just as happy producing articles titled 'In France on a Bicycle', or pursuing his mission work. But his archive of often unpublished photographs, as well as his meticulous preparatory notes for articles on houses, which include Pollok House in Glasgow, make this as yet uncatalogued archive one of the most significant accessions to the National Monuments Record's coverage of country houses in recent years. His grandson recalls that there was meant to be a northern companion to his *Lowlands* volume, but sadly the manuscript was destroyed by mistake following his death.

Hannan's photograph of the entrance hall shows that the tartan had by now spread cosily from the central ottoman to clothe the stone slabs shown in the British Rail photograph, and reveals the trophy of arms in the centre of the beamed ceiling, which has now lost its earlier antiquarian graining. The sale catalogue records that the 'life size' marble statues of Apollo and Venus were signed by Harwood and dated

Thomas Hannan's photographs of the dining room and drawing room show the quality of Baxter's elegant neo-classical plasterwork and the elegance of the furnishings, dispersed in the 1938 sale

1764 and stood on sienna and white-marble pedestals. There were several sets of hall chairs but only four had crests and part of the set was painted. The armour was extremely varied in its origins, with 'Two Turkish Yataghans (one of them found in the Citadel of Zante)', a pyramid of cannonballs from the Crimea and a 'Tomahawk Insc. Mr Forsyth Upper Canada 1793'.

Hannan's view of the dining room, set for lunch, is taken from the columned service end and shows how Baxter had to adapt the geometry of his ceiling designs to the irregularities of the ancient walls. The gilding of the ceiling seems to be in plain white, with no sign of its original picking out in grey, and must betray a nineteenth-century taste, as does the striped paper showing off the family portraits. The '18 old Mahogany chairs' were augmented by '9 Antique Mahogany ladderbacks' not in the photograph while

the 'two 5 foot carved and gilt console tables with white marble tops' may be those covered in white cloths on either side of the fireplace and matched the '9' 4" white and gilt shaped sideboard' with its 'Two Antique Mahogany wine urns'.

The final view shows a drawing room, entitled 'The Ballroom' on Baxter's plan, with a shaped end reflecting its bow window on the garden front. Again the ceiling seems to be gilded against a plain white ground rather than the colours mentioned in Smeaton's bill. The furniture illustrated shows the '7ft shaped back Setee in painted and gilt frame in Adam design' and its '8 shield back fauteuilles to match', and two of the '6 antique girandoles' hanging on the end wall. Unfortunately the photograph does not show the '4'4" very fine Adam shaped commode' or the 'Pair fine Adam gilt torcheres'. These must all be survivors from the first fitting-up

of this room or Duchess Jane's original smaller drawing room next to the dining room.

And so the list goes on and on with these telegraphic entries through floor after floor of the immense castle. One would give a lot today to see the 'Oil painting architectural subject attributed to Alexander' or the '4'6" Semi-circular console table on Carved and gilt Eagle Support. Marble Top inlaid Coat of Arms', which sound like survivors, perhaps

with a Florentine marble top, of the Second Duke's Italianate Baroque palace. By the time that Rupert Gunnis published his *Biographical Dictionary of British Sculptors*, in 1953, almost the entire collection of neo-classical sculpture from Gordon Castle and everything signed by Francis Harwood was in the stock of Messrs Crowthers of Isleworth; these photographs may help the collection to be traced today.

CHAPTER ELEVEN

Hawkhill

Edinburgh

A GEORGIAN GEM THAT THE CITY OF EDINBURGH FAILED TO SAVE

It would be difficult to think of a more perfect design for a relatively modest Scottish classical house than John Adam's Hawkhill Villa near Edinburgh – the quintessence of the eighteenth-century concept of the 'neat' – or one that has been more wantonly destroyed. It is included here as an example of a particularly vulnerable type, the urban, or perhaps more accurately suburban, villa; and the tale of its sad end also illustrates the increasing professionalism of the amenity societies that were formed after the Second World War to stem the tide of demolitions.

The villa was a popular Edinburgh type because the city was so relentlessly urban, confined by geography on such a steep narrow ridge that high-rise flats became the norm. In summer, with so many people crowded together, conditions were intolerable and, for those with means, the neo-classical ideal of a temporary escape from the cares of business to the real countryside was always seductive. The Scottish nobility and leading government officials had always favoured detached houses surrounded by their own pleasure grounds near the city and the success of the villa derived from its ready adaptability to more restricted budgets. The topography of the countryside near Edinburgh is exceptionally varied, with a sea coast bounded by hills, and villas tended to cluster along contour lines to exploit attractive views, the distant vision of Edinburgh dominated by the Castle Rock providing a favourite focus.

Hawkhill was designed in 1757 by John Adam for Andrew Pringle, Lord Alemoor, Solicitor-General for Scotland and celebrated for his courtroom oratory. The law court tied him to Edinburgh but Hawkhill, near Restalrig and next to Lochend Loch, with views across the Firth of Forth, provided escape and respite in periods of leisure. What makes Hawkhill exceptional is its Palladian perfection; Lord Alemoor's patronage inspired John Adam to create a restrained Edinburgh variation of an Italian casino or Parisian pavilion. Lord Alemoor was a bachelor, needing less space than a family would have, which allowed Adam to miniaturise and simplify its design.

Although John Adam's architecture can seem staid in comparison to the inventiveness of his brilliant younger brother, Robert, he had also inherited his

LEFT: The dining room at Hawkhill with its paintings by Delacour still *in situ* and a fine Adam chimney-piece; photo by George Nicol, March 1966

skills as a planner from his father, William, on whose relatively early death in 1748 he had to assume control of the family business. William Adam's genius for planning can be seen on a large scale in masterpieces like Hopetoun, where he had to shoehorn a great state apartment into Bruce's existing plan, and Duff House, which had intricately planned apartments, with their mezzanine closets serviced by spiral staircases and integral servants' rooms, but can also be seen in miniature in a studied group of small houses like Minto House in Edinburgh. At the time of William Adam's death in 1748, his many unfinished projects included his monumental publication *Vitruvius Scoticus*, which surveyed the classical buildings already realised in Scotland beginning with the Palace of Holyroodhouse, and was intended to publicise his own designs. Although this book was not published until 1811, by which time it had acquired an antiquarian interest, John Adam had many of the plates re-engraved during the 1760s to improve its presentation and took the opportunity to add designs of his own, including a handsome plate of Hawkhill. This was engraved by Mazell, and the plans and elevations are composed into an attractive pattern on the page entitled 'Lord Allemore's Villa at Hawkhill near Edinburgh' – an early Scottish use of the term 'villa'. John Adam also possessed an Edinburgh villa at North Merchiston and took pleasure in its improvement.

The skill of Hawkhill's design lies in its being not quite as simple as it appeared. The villa was entered through a Venetian door from the entrance steps, a feature later covered by an elegant glazed porch whose narrow glazing and elegant Pompeian colonettes suggest that it was an early Greek Revival addition. On the opposite façade, five large sash windows survey the sea view, of which three light the lofty rectangular dining room, with the remaining pair illuminating the square drawing room; both rooms also have windows in their end walls. The vestibule behind the entrance door takes the elegant form of an octagon leading axially to the dining room but, tucked into the angle on the left, and ingeniously lighted from the left-hand light beside the Venetian door, is a spiral service stair linking this miniature

LEFT: Entrance front of Hawkhill, with its elegant early-19th-century glazed porch protecting John Adam's Venetian doorway

View of the octagonal hall
on the piano nobile; the
central doorway leads to
the dining room

piano nobile to the basement kitchen, below the dining room, and the attic bedrooms above, which were
lit by skylights. Lord Alemoor's bedroom was on the
right of the octagonal vestibule, with a closet lit by
the right-hand light of the Venetian door, and bal-
anced by what may be his dressing room. All of these
rooms had chimney-pieces with flues in the central
transverse wall. These rooms were lower than the
two public rooms at the front of the house, to allow
for a mezzanine above with its rooms pleasingly
proportioned in relation to their smaller stature.

The quality of this intricate design was paralleled
by a meticulously high standard of execution,
characteristic of the Adams. There was fine rococo
plasterwork but the glory of Hawkhill was the
large dining room, which had a complete cycle of
decorative painting set in gilded frames with a square
over-mantel and overdoors interspersed with

elegant ovals, bearing landscapes reminiscent of
Gaspard Dughet, to create a convincing modern
Scottish version of the frescoed antique Roman
tricliniums. The chimney-piece, in grey marble, was
of a characteristic type from the Adams' marble
works and identical to similar examples at Duff
House and Dumfries House. This unusually polished
and complete scheme of decoration must have
continued to appeal to later generations and its
antique character was played up by a later Greek
Revival stencilled scheme reminiscent of Alexander
Thomson's decorations. The square drawing room,
however, was updated with an imposing black marble
Greek Revival chimney-piece, possibly suggesting
that the functions of these rooms were swapped
later.

Lord Alemoor died at Hawkhill in 1776 and his
villa continued to serve a succession of later owners

until the twentieth century. On Kirkwood's 1817 map of Edinburgh it is described as belonging to Mr Johnston of Alva and is shown surrounded by a miniature park with a serpentine walk round its perimeter. The map not only marks Lord Alemoor's 'Observatory' on the boundary nearest Edinburgh, but also shows a miniature sunk service court on the right-hand flank next to the kitchen – a feature characteristic of John Adam's architecture. But this generous villa-sized plot of land proved its undoing in the twentieth century, when urban pressures and the expansion of Edinburgh threatened Hawkhill's character and thus its viability as a home. The City of Edinburgh acquired the land as a recreation ground for the surrounding housing and unfortunately a bakery was built on ground below Hawkhill's entrance front. However, in 1966 the sea was still visible from the tall sashes of the rear façade, which now surveyed a 'sports ground' less happily ornamented by the 'charred skeleton of the games pavilion'. The City was attracted by the idea of using Hawkhill itself as a new games pavilion but, when this proved impractical, decided that it was essential to demolish the villa to extend the area of the sports ground itself.

They met with opposition. The Scottish Georgian Society was founded on 26 March 1956 by Eleanor Robertson, who felt 'that it was time to form a society which, by promoting interest in our Georgian architecture and town planning, might help to preserve them'. Its first case concerned the threat to Edinburgh's George Square, three sides of which the University of Edinburgh wanted to demolish to form a modern campus. With the support of older amenity societies, particularly the Cockburn Association, the Society pressed for a public enquiry (there may have been a certain creative tension, since Eleanor's husband, Professor Giles Robertson, happened to be the University's Professor of Fine Art). The success of her fledgling society owed everything to her gift for drawing able people into a worthy cause. In Colin McWilliam she found a most articulate case worker; few people in Scotland could rival his knowledge of Scotland's historic buildings after his many years of first-hand experience as

Director of the Scottish National Buildings Record, while through his architectural training he could often propose practical solutions to produce a workable compromise. A little later, in Alistair Rowan, then a young lecturer in Professor Robertson's Department, she found a no less able activities organiser and one whose pupils were inevitably also enjoyably drawn into assisting the society's work. It

Detail of the circular staircase, seen from the octagonal hall

was at Alistair Rowan's suggestion that James Simpson, then a young architectural student, started researching the history of William Adam's *Vitruvius Scoticus*; he soon found that Hawkhill's academic interest was overshadowed by the necessity to argue for its very survival.

Writing in the *Scotsman* in July 1966, in a campaigning article headlined 'Another Georgian House to Go: City's Approach to Heritage', Colin McWilliam gave a measured account of Hawkhill's significance, but the irony that its fate now lay in the hands of the City's 'Education Committee', responsible for recreation grounds, was not lost on him:

> Is this to be an obituary notice? . . . Will the inevitability of progress be invoked? Will the house be blamed for being behind a bakery or for having inconsiderately taken up space on its own grounds? Will it be claimed that a house of this obviously enjoyable quality can only be appreciated by antiquarians? I hope that time and ink will not be wasted on these hoary propositions.
>
> I still have a clear conception of what Hawkhill is and what it could be, a building serving a useful purpose, giving daily pleasure to the people of an unattractive part of Edinburgh and a rare experience (through all the ingenuity at the city's command) to the many visitors to whom this chapter of the Adam story is unknown. Some honour paid to our greatest architectural family will be a fine investment.

The Scottish Georgian Society did not give up easily. They canvassed for the re-erection of Hawkhill on a fresh site and then, with a grant from the Historic Buildings Council, arranged for both the recording and removal of the key components of its elegant interiors to enable them to be recreated elsewhere. It was at this time that the Scottish National Buildings Record made this photographic survey, in March 1966. Happily, the complete cycle of decorative paintings had been removed by 1971 to the safekeeping of The National Trust for Scotland's

conservation centre at Stenhouse Mansion, and thus escaped destruction when Hawkhill, after years of neglect and vandalism, was gutted by fire. Its obituary notice was finally published by James Simpson in the *Bulletin of the Scottish Georgian Society* in 1972. Understandably his account has a tone of wearied resignation at the pointless destruction by vandals of this attractive house, while taking some comfort from the partial salvation of the interiors because 'much of the significance of Hawkhill lay in the decoration of its principal apartments'. As a result of the Scottish Georgian Society's historical researches, the cycle of decorative painting was confidently attributed to William Delacour, who had certainly carried out the Watteauesque decorations in another of the Adams' elegant miniaturised villas, Lord Milton's house in the Canongate, and became very much part of the Adam circle; his finest surviving work must be the glorious antique landscape panels in the Saloon at Yester in 1761.

Both McWilliam's and Simpson's articles invoke a litany of other Edinburgh villas recently lost or currently threatened, including Newington, Warriston and Pilrig. It may be that Simpson's battle cry was a turning point in rethinking the need to preserve this aspect of Edinburgh's heritage, leading to the preservation of more fortunate villas; it certainly inspired me, as a young undergraduate, to write my dissertation on their origins and development. Because of their very proximity to the city, it was perhaps inevitable that urban expansion could only be at the expense of the villa grounds that encircled Edinburgh. Unlike country houses, villas tended to have a pattern of suiting the needs of a particular individual owner and rarely went down a line of family inheritance, so their individual histories were characterised by frequent changes of ownership and crises. Their lifeblood was views, policies and sufficient garden, and when that was lost they were abandoned. But the tragedy of Hawkhill is that its policies survived as a recreation ground and that the city did so little to save such a perfect jewel of a building, one that could have given 'daily pleasure' to so many in an area of Edinburgh that is less attractive without it.

Few people in Scotland have made a more

inspiring contribution to architectural conservation than James Simpson. Looking back on Hawkhill after thirty years, he feels that at that time one simply could not expect the City to care about a building by John Adam, and this shows how much thinking has changed. He adds that although the samples of interior detail were carefully saved and preserved in the City's furniture store, at the time of local government reorganisation these precious records were, sadly, disposed of. But the painted canvases are now stored in the City Art Centre and Simpson hopes that they may find a new setting in the restored Great Dining Room at Mavisbank, which has very similar proportions and an appropriate villa ethos.

Detail of the lively Rococo plasterwork of the original drawing-room ceiling with palm fronds and flowers

CHAPTER TWELVE

Balbardie

West Lothian

ONE OF ROBERT ADAM'S
LAST WORKS IS LOST

Robert Adam is Scotland's most celebrated architect. His plain Scotch surname is synonymous with architectural elegance throughout the world and few architects have given their name to such a readily recognisable style.

If one were to judge only from the large number of his buildings listed in the Demolition File of the National Monuments Record of Scotland, one might assume that the Scots had been rather careless with his reputation. Dalquharran, a miniature essay in his castle style with a skied circular library, designed for his niece and her husband in 1790, has now lost its interiors, as has the gutted contemporary Archerfield, which once had a cycle of particularly elegant reception rooms around a domed circular tribune. The diminutive Barholm, in a remote part of Scotland, and which rather strayed from his careful working drawings of 1788, went in 1960. The triangular Walkinshaw of 1791 has gone too. And the list goes relentlessly on with Alva, Jerviston and Maudsley, culminating in the quite unforgivable demolition, as recently as 1973, of the College Street Buildings at 179–185 High Street, Glasgow, designed by James Adam in 1793 to accommodate the academic staff of Glasgow University. This large number of entries in the demolitions lists, however, may merely represent his proportionate share; his Scottish patrons were to keep Adam constantly on the road north, especially during his final years.

There is thus a depressingly wide choice of demolished Adam country houses for this chapter but I have chosen Balbardie in West Lothian because its celebrity as an Adam design was home-grown and thus predated the scholarship that radiated from the John Soane Museum in London, where Adam's office drawings have ended up. It has the poignant additional interest of having been designed in the last weeks of the architect's life before his death on 3 March 1792 and demonstrates that his ability to tackle fresh architectural challenges remained undimmed to the end.

This elegiac photographic study of the unusually architectonic apsidal links between the wings of Balbardie and the main house, from the archives of the Royal Incorporation of Architects in Scotland, is a tribute to an early twentieth-century Scottish interest in Adam. Although a mere detail, the photograph possesses an aesthetic completeness, summing up the elegance of Adam's architectural language, with the elegant geometry decorated with beribboned

LEFT: Entrance front of Balbardie, photographed by Colin McWilliam in 1954 before demolition

festoons and a suave vase borne aloft by the columns of the exedral screen. This photographic record must have been inspired by the presence, in the same archive, of Adam's own presentation design for Balbardie, which the Incorporation generously returned to the descendants of his patron, Alexander Marjoribanks, in the early 1980s. The photograph is still accompanied by two measured drawings, signed by Henry F. Kerr and dated 1913, to show the way these apsidal recesses are sculpted into the front elevation.

It was not Kerr himself but a fellow architect, Thomas Purves Marwick, who published Balbardie in the *Architectural Review* in October 1920. At this time the *Review* was as interested in historical buildings and decoration as modern architectural designs. Marwick's interest was professional because Balbardie was an early example of a Scottish country house that had passed into institutional ownership and lost its domestic purpose through the pressures

of industrialisation from nearby Bathgate. Although Groome's *Ordnance Gazetteer of Scotland* in 1901 could write that the 'hilly grounds to the NE, and the beautiful park of Balbardie on the N, give a cheerful aspect to the town', by 1920 Marwick could only lament that the outlook from the house was blocked by 'a mountain of pit refuse' and a long series of 'railway wagons creeping over the green fields'. Bathgate had become a boom town through the coming of the railway in 1849 and then, in 1850, the local strata of black bituminous shale was found to be unusually rich in mineral oil that could be exploited for the production of gas and paraffin. In 1861 the Balbardie estate was purchased by Daniel Stewart's College in Edinburgh for investment and they applied its revenues to the school's educational purposes. Daniel Stewart's College was one of the charitable schools managed by the Merchant Company of Edinburgh and Marwick not only designed their Hall in Hanover Street, which was

The south front of Balbardie in 1954

OPPOSITE: Detail of the exedral screen linking the pavilions to the principal block, showing the exceptionally fine polished ashlar stonework

completed in 1901, but also became its Assistant Master of the Company in 1917.

Marwick's article reproduces Adam's original designs for the front and back elevations, signed in London and dated 1792, and records that these had been lent for reproduction by the Reverend George Marjoribanks, whose father was the eighteenth of Alexander Marjoribanks' nineteen children. The Incorporation's photographic study of the apse by an uncredited photographer was obviously taken for this article, and it also reproduces a study of the main elevation. Marwick responded particularly enthusiastically to the beauty of the two apses, which he thought more typical of Adam's interior architecture: 'They are really beautiful designs, reminiscent of the apse, or tribune in Roman Basilica, while the masonry is as sharp and as well preserved as on the day it was chiselled.' In the photograph the finesse of the stonework is enhanced by the smoked effect, showing up the grain of each individual ashlar block, like the figure of some prized exotic marble, although in reality this was an unfortunate side effect of Bathgate's rapid industrialisation.

The photograph of the central portion of the house is rather less comfortable in its detailing and it is clear that neither of the Adam brothers lived to supervise the execution of their drawings. A working drawing for the entrance on the North Front in the Soane Museum is dated 'Edinburgh 10th May 1793' but it is possible that it took some years to build. A photograph of the rear of this central block in 1953 is surprising because the façade, unusually, is an even four bays wide, thus presenting an unresolved duality, rather than the conventional number of five proposed in the 1792 design. The way in which the outer lights of Adam's proposed Venetian windows in each apse have been reduced to uncomfortably spaced narrow slits also suggests a lack of meticulous supervision. These infelicities were surely the result of a decision by the patron to retain the central part of the existing house on the site. In *The Bathgate Book* (2001), the editors, William Hendrie and Allister Mackie, include a description of this earlier house, which had seven rooms with hearths in 1691. But like the grit in the oyster that produces the pearl, it

was probably the recasting of the earlier house that led to Adam's inventive solution of the apses.

Marjoribanks was descended from an early Lord Provost of Edinburgh and the occasion for a new house must have arisen from his marriage to Catherine Laurie of Polmont in 1790. Margaret Sanderson published the account book that survives from Robert Adam's last visit to Scotland in 1791 in *Architectural History*, volume 25 (1982), and it reveals his almost frenetic journeying around his native land. Adam visited Balbardie on 30 May and returned, after calling at his new house at Newliston, also in West Lothian, on 23 August. The account book records the receipt of thirty guineas 'from Mr Marjoribanks on Account' on 25 November which may relate to the preparation of drawings.

There are no existing plans to accompany Adam's elevations, but Marwick's article does reproduce modern survey plans. These reveal that the main stair rose to the right of the central block, immediately behind the windows of this façade. The geometric service stair lay behind the right-hand exedra. There was an apsidally ended dining room on the ground floor of the central block to the rear on the left. Perhaps because of the position of these stairs, corridors ran along the front of the building connecting the wings, through the exedral link buildings, to the central block. The exedral solution must have been to create an integrated design where the accommodation in the wings was readily accessible from the central rooms, whereas, in a more conventional Adam and Palladian composition, the link buildings would surely not have risen higher than a single storey, giving a more varied silhouette. The integration of the paired wings with their link buildings into the central portion of the house could have produced rather a monumental block-like effect, but the setting back of the link buildings and the sculptural scooping out of their exedras gives that 'movement' to the design that Adam so desired. To the very end of his career Adam's inventive streak was at his best when responding to the constraints of existing buildings. The plans also show that the kitchen was in the right-hand wing – suggesting the dining-room apse was for the sideboard recess, and

the house continued in a single-storey wing screening a surprisingly circular office court.

The Soane Museum Adam drawings also include inventive, and sadly unexecuted, sketch plans and elevations for what their cataloguer has entitled a 'Castellated Tearoom' for Alexander Marjoribanks. These comprise a staircase tower at the rear rising behind the circular structure to lead to a first-floor room, with its windows giving on to a balcony and with a viewing platform on the flat roof above this. One of the designs envisaged the building as an ancient ruin with timeworn crumbling blocks of stone and the criss-crossed balcony railings taking

the form of rough timbers, as though in a rough and ready repair.

The more recent history of Balbardie has been ever more unhappy. In 1920 Marwick felt that the house had 'fallen on evil times' and the 'withdrawal of the supporting strata has caused somewhat serious fractures' in the structure. The house was then divided up into accommodation for the farm workers from the nearby Mains of Balbardie, with the apses altered to porches with access doors. He published photographs of two of the chimney-pieces, one with a fine early stove grate but the other containing two flat brass ornaments of shire horses perched on the grate

Detail of fireplace on first floor, with a miniature stove range and gas lighting bracket installed for agricultural tenants

Detail of frieze over principal stair with tottering vases and bucrania

bars, presumably a decorative addition reflecting the interests of the farm labourers.

In 1953 Colin McWilliam was able to make a final, and very inadequate photographic record of Balbardie before most of it was demolished in 1956. It was presumably because it was already divided in a tenement, and possibly also reflecting the undermining of the structure, that the right-hand wing was initially kept standing, although McWilliam marked up the photographs on the SNBR mounts, lettered in his distinctive penmanship, to explain this astonishingly brutal amputation.

McWilliam was also on site in time to record something of the interior. His photos include a fuzzy detail of the plaster frieze over the main stair with bucrania alternating with almost tottering vases, heavily silted up with institutional whitewash. His photograph of a room with canted corners shows a jaunty cheap lodging-house wallpaper, while another

photograph of a fine composition chimney-piece decorated with vases shows the ad hoc insertion of a cooking range and a gas light at one end of the chimney-shelf, as Balbardie sank through the social scale indoors as a result of the loss of its grounds.

The surviving wing was in turn demolished in 1975 but lingered on for some years as a ruin. Although several neo-classical architects enjoyed making fanciful drawings of how their buildings would look at a distant point as ruins and Adam himself had enjoyed the caprice of a ruined castellated tea-house at Balbardie, it would be difficult to conceive of anything less picturesque than this shattered ruin as recorded in the final photographs taken by West Lothian Council. Daubed with painted slogans and with the lintel of the exedral frieze hanging perilously both columnless and vaseless, it seems to cry 'put me out of my misery please'. The site is now the Balbardie Park of Peace.

Detail of geometrically
shaped room on ground
floor

CHAPTER THIRTEEN

Rosneath

Dumbartonshire

LORNIAN PALACE
ON THE FIRTH OF CLYDE

Kitty Cruft's sad 1961 photograph of the dark disintegrating ruin of the great neo-classical palace of Rosneath, louring over a regimented line of diminutive light-coloured streamlined caravans like the carcase of a stranded whale on a holiday beach, must be amongst the most poignant images to document the doom of the country house in post-war Scotland.

The caravan site had been attracted by the same picturesque backdrop that had been celebrated in the design of the palace. Sited near the southern extremity of the slender finger-like Rosneath peninsula that projected into the Firth of Clyde between Dunoon and Helensburgh, it enjoyed all-round views of some of the most spectacular scenery in Scotland, fretted into innumerable snaking sea lochs.

But this picturesque version of Rosneath had its origins in the no less ill-starred end of the earlier Rosneath Castle, an ancient stronghold of the Argylls, which was lost in a fire on 30 May 1802. When the castle was fitted out in 1630 by the Marquis of Argyll, it was the strategic possibilities of the peninsula that were paramount. Rosneath was always to be a secondary seat to the family's main stronghold at Inveraray, on the more remote Loch Fyne, but the architectural history of the two castles was inevitably interlinked. When the Third Duke of Argyll employed Roger Morris in 1744 to rebuild Inveraray in a pioneering Gothick Revival mode, Morris also made Gothick designs for Rosneath. Although this Gothick style was perfectly attuned to the rugged Highland scenery, the Fifth Duke of Argyll and his Duchess, one of the beautiful Gunning sisters, employed Robert Mylne to transform the interior during the 1780s into a dazzling homage to Marie Antoinette's Paris. In pursuit of this sparkling Francophile chic, Mylne orchestrated the interior framework for the tapestries and works of art, which were directly commissioned in Paris; French decorative painters and workmen resident in England and Scotland were also employed, and helped to train a native workforce in French luxury trades like furniture gilding.

Mylne was also asked to make more humdrum improvements at Rosneath, which retained something of the air of a genuine ancient stronghold in comparison with fashionable modern Inveraray. Rosneath, sited on a terrace above the coastline, had a unique silhouette where a pair of symmetrically matched

LEFT: The entrance front of Rosneath with Bonomi's five-columned *porte cochère*, photographed by Kitty Cruft before its demolition in 1961

View of the rear façade with pilaster stumps of the unbuilt circular portico

round towers on the principal façade were continued up into abstract drums of masonry whose scale was further underlined in the contrast between these soaring towers and a diminutive block of office buildings on the shoreline.

It was thus to the trusted Mylne that the ageing Duke turned for advice after the fire, and writing from London in September 1802, Mylne was pleased to learn that, while the site was to be maintained, there would be no attempt to restrict the new plan to the old internal partition walls and foundations. He asked the Duke if the new Rosneath was to 'maintain and support the character of a Castellated house . . . or the private Mansion of a Personage in Retirement?' and produced plans for a relatively modest house.

But in the event Mylne was to be passed over in the creation of the new house because the Duke's heir, the Marquess of Lorne, who resided at Rosneath, had a more ambitious dream palace in mind. Shortly before the fire, the Duke, who was an enthusiastic exponent of the latest ideas for agricultural improvement, had commissioned a new court of farm offices, which were designed by the artist Alexander Nasmyth, who, as Janet Cooksey writes in her definitive 1991 biography of him, had considerable experience of painting picturesque landscapes in which the (imaginary) buildings were at one with their setting. The magnificent scenery of the Rosneath Peninsula inspired Nasmyth to transform the circular court of farm buildings into a Gothick extravaganza with crenellated turrets surrounding a high tower with a fretwork parapet, on such an extravagant scale that it would be equally at home in Catherine the Great's Russia. *The General View of the Agriculture of Dumbarton*, in 1811, judged that these farm buildings were 'obviously designed for ornament, at least as much for use, and consequently, are constructed on a plan much too expensive for imitation'.

Nasmyth was on hand at Rosneath to record the smoking ruins of the Castle on 31 May 1802. Perhaps inevitably, the new building was to take a similar course to the farm buildings and a fresh site was soon selected to maximise the picturesque opportunities. Nasmyth prepared both an oil painting and a watercolour of the new house to show it in its intended setting, and, probably at the Marquess of Lorne's instigation, the architect Joseph Bonomi was selected to realise Nasmyth's designs. Bonomi had been born in Italy and brought to London by Robert and James Adam to serve in their office. He has the additional distinction of being mentioned by Jane Austen in *Sense and Sensibility*. But Bonomi's architecture was to be rather more challengingly original than these biographical details might otherwise suggest, as can be seen in the eccentricity of its entrance portico with its uneven number of five Ionic columns bearing flaring volutes, with the axis blocked by the central column to underline that it was a *porte cochère* for carriages to drive through, an idea continued in the equally awkward pairs of three columns that advanced to frame the end bays of the entrance façade.

The plan of the new house had a similar clarity, with a broad transverse corridor that led to all the rooms and a double family apartment, with private suites of rooms for both the Duke and the Marquess on either side of the entrance hall that lay behind the *porte cochère*. The central corridor served a chain of five public rooms on the opposite side of the house; this would normally have been the garden front but here all the rooms enjoyed magnificent views and the corner rooms had windows in two sides. The central reception room broke forward in a circular bow and this geometry was to have continued outward into the landscape in a circular portico with unusual

paired columns. The bow would have continued upwards to resolve in a circular pavilion rising high above the roofline to provide a panorama room where the all-round views could be enjoyed in comfort through its great arched windows. This skied pavilion may have taken its cue from the drum towers of the original house and certainly recalled its dramatic silhouette; Bonomi in his drawings referred to it as the building on the roof. Its visual impact would have been enhanced by the firm horizontal to be established through the sinking of the basement storey into a fosse that recalls a characteristic feature of Gothick Inveraray, and by the concealment of the third attic storey and its dormer windows behind an encircling parapet.

It is not surprising that only part of this grand

Detail of the disintegrating plasterwork, exposed to the elements, of one of the pair of apses in the library

Marquess succeeded his father as Sixth Duke of Argyll; he focused more on Inveraray, and building work at Rosneath slowed. Bonomi himself died in 1808, after exhibiting a perspective view of the entrance front at the Royal Academy in 1806 showing the rooftop rotunda levitating above the flat balustraded roofline like a heliport. Throughout the construction the Fifth Duke had fretted to his son about his fear that 'Two houses of Expence' would ruin the family; that Lord Lorne would find that Nasmyth and Bonomi would prove 'Expensive Pets' but most of all about the slight to poor Mylne after so many years of his devoted careful stewardship that had always been in the Duke's 'Pecuniary Interest'. (In fact, the Duke's fears were not realised, and in October 1877, when a catastrophic fire broke out at Inveraray, the Eighth Duke remarked that it was fortunate they had another castle to go to during the restoration process.)

The house's unusual aesthetic qualities and its general state of unfinishedness were encapsulated in the description in *Rosneath Past and Present* (1893):

> A spacious corridor extends from one end of the building to the other, off which the large public rooms open, from each of which there is a beautiful view. The rooms are very lofty and handsomely proportioned, and have decorated friezes on the upper portions of the walls and ceilings. One exceedingly elegant room is the circular library under the tower, with stone walls and classic ceiling decorations – a finely designed apartment. Down stairs, the kitchen is of great size, with various other vaulted halls and rooms; several of these at the east end of the castle being unfinished and used for storing plants, containing also a considerable portion of the stone balustrades and other ornaments of the exterior. The upper part of the castle has a number of large bedrooms, all plainly fitted up, for there is little splendour in any of the internal furnishings. A few family portraits – one recently added, a full-length picture of the Marquess of Lorne, and an engraving of the beautiful Miss Gunning, adorn the public

design was actually completed. The circular portico was never even erected, giving the continued bow the conventional effect of a tower rather than the floating skied pavilion that had been intended. Just as with the Gothick farm offices, the design proved too expensive to realise in its entirety. In 1806 the

rooms, and two handsome alabaster vases in the Library will attract attention. But want of funds compelled the abandonment of the original design, and only the north part of the castle was completed according to the architect's plan.

Kitty Cruft's photographs capture the noble scale and sheer grandeur of the central cross-vaulted corridor even in its decrepitude, showing how it was approached through Bonomi's favourite device of a Diocletian screen of Doric columns, and lit by huge circular-headed end windows which followed the line of the vault. Bonomi's working drawings identify the line of five public rooms as the music room and the drawing room on the left of the central circular library in the bow and then with the billiard room – a requirement of the Duke's – and the dining room on the right. There is a particularly dramatic photograph of one of the pair of apses in the library showing what little remained of Bonomi's ornamental vocabulary, surprisingly lamely Adamesque in its ribbons, festoons and Vitruvian scrollwork, still just clinging to laths that were now exposed to the elements and sea air.

On his design for the entrance arch 'of the subterraneous Street leading to the East Court of the new House', another of this House's more unusual intended features, Bonomi included a tablet inscribed 'LORNIAN PALACE', and the Palace was to attract a very real princess when Princess Louise, the most beautiful and artistic of Queen Victoria's daughters, married the Marquess of Lorne in 1871, the first daughter of a reigning sovereign to marry a commoner since 1515. Lord Lorne succeeded his father as Ninth Duke of Argyll in 1900, but he died in 1914 and Rosneath became the Princess's dower house during her long widowhood; during the First World War she gave it over to convalescing officers. It was through the patronage of the Princess, who herself had trained as a sculptress, that Lutyens was employed to make additions to the Ferry Inn at Rosneath in 1896 (Gertrude Jekyll ticked the Princess off for wasting her protégé's valuable time on less architectural pursuits).

The Princess and the Ninth Duke were childless and he was succeeded by their nephew, the Tenth

Duke. Her death in 1939 precipitated his sale of the contents of Rosneath, held on the premises by Dowells of Edinburgh between 7 and 11 October 1940; their sale catalogue includes a handsome view not only of the five-columned *porte cochère* wreathed in ivy but also of the Princess's drawing room. This

ABOVE AND OPPOSITE: Views down the central corridor, lit by a circular-headed window at each end

View through the screen
separating the entrance
hall from the transverse
corridor

shows an awkward attempt to Early Georgianise
Bonomi's austerities with a deep plaster frieze,
broken pediments over the doors, a vaguely Inigo
Jones chimney-piece and a fashionably high dado. But
this was surely intended merely as a background
to harmonise with the Princess's superb antique
furnishings. This room had a 'fine Savonnerie Carpet,
floral and scroll designs in colours, on dark brown
and blue ground . . .' and the catalogue also includes
a photo of a superb Moorfields carpet from the
dining room, also described as a Savonnerie. These
carpets date from the time of Inveraray's fitting-out,
making one wonder if they began life there, like a
pair of 'Adam' firescreens also individually illustrated, along with a set of tapestry panels of the oft-
woven Loves of the Gods. Soon afterwards the Tenth
Duke had to put up the house itself for sale, bitterly
lamenting the loss of lands that his family had held
'since 1470'.

Without the Princess's attractive contents,
Rosneath must have been too gaunt for any future
domestic use. During the war, in a final reversion
to its earlier strategic importance, it was used
for military exercises, and in 1942 Churchill,
Eisenhower and Montgomery planned Operation
Torch, the successful invasion of French North
Africa, within its walls. After the war its grounds
took on a new role, exploiting its scenic attractions,
as a caravan park. There seems to have been an idea
that the public rooms might support this new use
but, as the house deteriorated, it inevitably became a
dangerous adventure playground for children and
this was to seal its fate, leading to its demolition in
1961. The Scottish National Buildings Record had
several photographic campaigns before this end but,
as Kitty Cruft recalls, 'it was impossible to save when
nobody had heard of Bonomi'. The *Scotsman* was
there at the photo-finish, headlined 'ROSNEATH

CASTLE DISAPPEARS IN DUST', for the final explosive moment with blocks of its fine Garscube stonework tumbling in the smoke, and recorded that '200 lb. of gelignite ended the history of the building'.

A handsome pair of enriched white marble Adamesque chimneypieces had been salvaged and these were reset in the saloon at Inveraray in place of two plain nineteenth-century chimney-pieces as a very modest souvenir of this monster house. When Ian Lindsay and Mary Cosh published their *Inveraray and the Dukes of Argyll* (1973), one of the finest monographs on any British country house, they, perhaps understandably, took a rather frosty view of the eccentricity and extravagance that had characterised the secondary seat in comparison with the perfections of the principal seat and its planned model

town on the shores of Loch Fyne; they acknowledged that 'it was, in its own way, as original a design as Inveraray itself' but quoted Summerson's opinion of Bonomi's architecture as possessing 'a marked insensibility'. But looking back now, almost fifty years after its demolition, it is difficult not to feel a pang of regret for a house whose design had so fully responded to the resplendent surrounding scenery of the Firth of Clyde and whose sublimity had so boldly striven to live up to one of the finest views in Scotland, which it sought to capture in the kind of living three-dimensional panorama that so gripped the imagination of early-nineteenth-century artists. How thrilling it would be to ascend the balustraded platform on the leads above the floating rotunda on a fine day with a map, to work out how far one could see!

View of Princess Louise's drawing room, from the 1940 sale catalogue

CHAPTER FOURTEEN

Kelvingrove

Glasgow

CONSUMMATELY ELEGANT VILLA, SACRIFICED TO MUSEUM EXPANSION

By the mid-nineteenth century, photography had been recognised as an ideal medium for the recording of buildings, and among the glories of early Scottish photography were those by Annan of Glasgow. *The Old Country Houses of the Old Glasgow Gentry* is one of their classic works and this photograph of Kelvingrove comes from the 1878 edition. It was a timely record; then the second city of the British Empire, Glasgow and its housing stock were undergoing enormous change as a result of the huge influx of wealth from imperial trade.

This image of the villa of Kelvingrove, clearly taken in winter, has a raw quality, with the rather institutional benches facing different ways, the scrubby shrubs or tiny trees in the foreground and, most unusually, the figure of a man near the right-hand side of the façade. All these eccentricities are at odds with the elegantly playful inventiveness of the architecture itself with its bowed centre-piece, the giant Diocletian Venetian windows, apparently extending through both stories of the pavilions, and the façade brought to a fine finish with a trio of vases along the parapet.

The accompanying text reveals that Kelvingrove, no longer in domestic use, was an early example of a Scottish country house finding an unusual new function:

> Kelvingrove has now (mainly by the exertions of Bailie McBean) been converted into a valuable museum. One wing has been removed, and on its site a large addition built, which dwarfs what remains of the fine old mansion of the Colquhouns, the Pattisons and the Dennistouns.

The photograph does not show this modern wing, which was erected in 1876.

According to the text, Kelvingrove's site, near the West End of the city and on the banks of the River Kelvin, had been purchased by Patrick Colquhoun in 1782, the year he became Lord Provost of Glasgow. Colquhoun, a dynamic man who established the Chamber of Commerce, built the house and gave it the characteristically bucolic villa name of 'Kelvingrove'. When his activities took him away from Glasgow his new house was advertised for sale in 1790 as 'The villa and lands of Kelvingrove, beautifully situated on the banks of the Kelvin, and perfectly retired, although within one mile of the city of Glasgow.'

LEFT: Annan's photograph shows the villa with its early-19th-century wings, before the addition of a new museum wing by the city architect in 1876

The sale notice, published in *Glasgow Past and Present* (1884), goes on to list its charms. The house overlooked the river and had a dining room, a drawing room and eight bedrooms with the usual cellarage and offices housing horses, cows, pigeons and poultry. There was a wash house and a 'commodious cold bath'. Shrubberies screened both the garden and the offices to preserve the purity of the prospect from the house. The brick garden walls were threaded with flues to force fruit trees. In 1792 Kelvingrove was purchased by John Pattison, a manufacturer, who was to enlarge its park with the purchase of a further twelve acres.

By the second half of the nineteenth century, Kelvingrove, not unreasonably given its striking elegance, was confidently attributed to Robert Adam. Of course, it is now obvious that Kelvingrove cannot be Adam's, and the Glasgow architect David Hamilton seems a more likely designer. It is difficult to reconcile the modesty of the 1790s sale notice with the splendid mansion in the photograph and – on purely visual grounds – it looks like a classic case of a modest small box of a villa being aggrandised through the addition of a pair of large public rooms on either end of the box. The interior view of the top of the stair certainly shows an Adamesque ceiling, but the deep frieze is more Regency in spirit, like the Pompeian colonettes leading back into the lower attic storey of the original building.

Although very little is known of Hamilton's early career, three volumes of his drawings survive in the collection of Glasgow University Library and include copies of Adam designs which led Sir Howard Colvin, in his standard *Biographical Dictionary of British Architects* (1954), to conclude that Hamilton must have had some early connection with the Adams' firm. Two plans in Volume 1 of his drawings, Numbers 135 and 136, show a similar proposal by an unknown architect to extend a diminutive three-bay box by the addition of a central bow containing the stair and larger wings at each end to supply a withdrawing room and dining room respectively. These extensions are integrated into a flawless composition embracing the existing villa, with a consummate skill and mastery in the handling of complex wall-planes and the whole tied together with strong

horizontals. The patron of these additions may have been John Pattison, who owned Kelvingrove from 1792 until 1806, or Richard Dennistoun, another Glasgow merchant, who purchased it from Pattison and whose family remained there until 1841.

By the mid-nineteenth century Glasgow had expanded to encompass Kelvingrove, and the city authorities bought both house and land, converting the former into a museum. But from the outset it was ill at ease in this handsome domestic setting. Looking back on its institutional history in *Municipal Glasgow: Its Evolution and Enterprises* (1914), James Paton, the Superintendent of the Art Galleries and Museums service, wrote, 'from the very first it was clear that the building was wholly unsuited for museum purposes . . . being far too small' and the 'limited space was subject to very severe strain'. Although it began as an industrial museum, a flood of generous gifts swelled the collections so that they soon embraced natural history, ethnology, art and antiquarian material.

To cope with this largesse, in 1874 the city architect John Carrick designed the new wing mentioned earlier, which, funded largely by public subscription, was opened in 1876. But this was merely a temporary improvement and for Paton, frustratingly, 'the space available made it quite impossible for any systematic classification or arrangement of its contents to be carried out, and it came ultimately to be looked on more as a store than a museum suited for educational or scientific purposes'. Nevertheless, he had to concede: 'Yet it cannot be doubted that, in some small measure, it suited both these ends, and there are many who, to this day, remember it affectionately as the parent of its more pretentious successor.'

This charm is ably conveyed by Annan's photograph, reproduced here, showing what must be a first-floor landing lying behind the central Venetianed windowed bow, where geometrical plasterwork and Pompeian colonettes formed an unusually elegant background to the densely crowded display of natural history specimens.

From 1883, the Museums and Galleries Committee had organised successful exhibitions in the halls of the bath houses and wash houses of the

Gorbals. These were so popular that when there was no suitable hall in the Bridgeton district, a branch museum was built on Glasgow Green and christened the People's Palace. This was followed in 1894 by a further branch museum in Camphill House, the grounds of which, like Kelvingrove, had been purchased to be a district municipal park.

Encouraged by these successes, which must have highlighted the continuing inadequacy of Kelvingrove, it was decided to hold a temporary exhibition in the latter's grounds in 1888. This made a profit of £46,000 for a new building. The Exhibition Association then offered to double this amount by public subscription if the city would grant a site for a new building in Kelvingrove park and, after an architectural competition, the present Kelvingrove Art Gallery and Museum, designed by J. W. Simpson and Milner Allen of London, with sculpture by Sir George Frampton, was opened in 1901 as the centrepiece of an even grander International Exhibition. In this mood of euphoria, the original Kelvingrove faded from sight:

> The exigencies of the exhibition demanded the demolition of Kelvingrove house, in which the nucleus of the museum was formed. That building, not devoid of romantic and poetical associations, and moreover a charming example of eighteenth century architecture in the Adam style, was taken down in 1899, and to that extent Kelvingrove museum was dismembered. As a separate institution it entirely ceased to exist at the close of the year 1900, when the wing which had been built by public subscription was denuded of its contents, and handed over to the exhibition authorities for their purposes.

After serving as the Japanese Pavilion, this wing, which had lingered like the smile on the Cheshire cat, was in turn excised. Perilla and Juliet Kinchin in their *Glasgow's Great Exhibitions* suggest that protests against the demolition of Kelvingrove villa held up preparations for the 1901 Great Exhibition. Newspaper reports of the council meeting at which Kelvingrove's fate was decided record that the lack of written evidence for the Adam attribution sealed its fate.

The great affection in which the modern Art Gallery and Museum at Kelvingrove is held by the citizens of Glasgow is perhaps some compensation for the loss of this charming villa, but writing in 1981 in *The City That Disappeared*, Frank Worsdall, who cared deeply for the City's architectural heritage through a darker period than now, held that: 'The demolition of Kelvingrove, one of Robert Adam's most original designs, is an example of that vandalism which is now characteristic of Glasgow.'

Annan's photograph of the staircase of Kelvingrove with its elegant Adamesque plasterwork and Pompeian colonettes, in use as a museum with crowded natural history specimens and a stuffed camel in the stairwell

Dunglass

East Lothian

NASMYTH'S ESSAY IN THE PICTURESQUE, SET IN THE LAMMERMUIRS

Though Dunglass's fate was to be blown up in 1958, it at least had the good luck to be photographed in its prime in 1925 by *Country Life*, and this fine visual record enables posterity to appreciate its importance in Scottish architectural history.

The *Country Life* article was written by the young Christopher Hussey, who had joined the magazine in 1921, and its first paragraph reflects his excitement at rediscovering the principles of the Picturesque aesthetic, as expounded by Uvedale Price, by which buildings were sited and designed in sympathy with their particular landscape settings. This thinking had influenced Hussey's own ancestors in choosing a situation for their new house at Scotney in Kent, where it could take full advantage of the view across to their ancient castle, now preserved as a romantic ruin. He was delighted to find that there was still a copy of *Sir Uvedale Price on the Picturesque* on the shelves of his grandfather's library at Scotney.

The patron at Dunglass, who must have been fired with the same enthusiasm in 1807, was Sir James Hall of Dunglass, who was imbued with the intellectual questioning that was to be so characteristic of Edinburgh during the Enlightenment, when it was known as the 'Modern Athens'. His principal interest was geology, an Edinburgh speciality, and, unusually, he tested his theories in practical laboratory experiments, rising to become President of the Royal Society of Edinburgh. In 1776 Sir James inherited the Dunglass estate, which his family had held since 1680. He was an enthusiastic amateur of architecture and the poor condition of the existing house at Dunglass gave him the opportunity to develop his interest in Picturesque theories by planning the new house to take full advantage of the estate's dramatic scenery near Cockburnspath, where the Lammermuir hills come down to the sea. The new house was to be perched at the edge of the deep ravine known as the Dunglass Dean, cut down the years by the Dunglass Burn.

Sir James had travelled on the continent during the early 1780s and in Italy met the artist Alexander Nasmyth, who named his son, who was to become the brilliant engineer and inventor, after Sir James. In keeping with Picturesque theory, Sir James entrusted Nasmyth with the selection of the site and overall appearance of the new Dunglass. Two of Nasmyth's preliminary sketch designs

LEFT: *Country Life*'s distant view of Dunglass from across the ravine, showing the Belvedere Room high above the body of the house

survive in the National Gallery of Scotland. Both are for scenographic machicolated castles, dramatically depicted from below, and thus reflecting the proposed site on the edge of the ravine. One sketch has flights of stairs plunging down to link garden terraces, while the other has a formidable-looking gatehouse. These Gothic designs, reflecting Sir James's enthusiasm for that style, may have been intended to recall the early history of the estate as one of the great border strongholds of the Homes; it was besieged by the English during the early years of Mary Queen of Scots' reign and finally blown up when held by the Covenanters. Hussey suggested that this castellated solution for the new Dunglass may have been given up because Sir James felt there was sufficient ancientness surviving on the estate by the 'very perfect relic of Scottish ecclesiastical architecture' a few yards from the front door: the collegiate church, which for centuries had been the burial place of the Earls of Home.

The artist was paid 'for a model of the house' and it is fascinating to contrast the intricacy of the final plan and silhouette of Dunglass with the monumentally simple classicism that Nasmyth had deemed suitable for the very different scenery at Rosneath (see Chapter 13). The new house was built between 1807 and 1813 under the supervision of the architect Richard Crichton, who had begun his career in the Adam office. Although there were elements of Dunglass that were Adamitic and must derive from Crichton, notably the carriage sweep to the Ionic colonnade on the surprisingly symmetrical entrance front, the drama of the composition owed more to a new Picturesque enthusiasm for the architecture of Sir John Vanbrugh.

Hussey felt the rather extraordinary cupolas of the dairy wing – in 1920 they covered the milk store and wash-house – were 'copied from the back regions of Castle Howard'. The tower rose to the many-windowed 'Belvedere Room', as it is entitled on the 1920 plans, which floated high above the body of the house and recalled the prospect rooms that were such a feature of both Nasmyth's mansion house and the farm offices at Rosneath. In J.P. Neale's *Views of the Seats of the Noblemen and Gentlemen in England, Wales, Scotland and Ireland* (1823) there is a description of the view from the Belvedere Room: 'A magnificent view of the ocean is to be had from the highest part of the edifice; including also a fine diversity of wooded grounds, and the pleasing prospects which a well cultivated district affords.'

Unfortunately there is nothing in this eclectic architectural language that drew on Sir James's enthusiasm for Gothic architecture. Developing the idea that the characteristic forms of Greek temples must have derived from archaic timber prototypes, Sir James set out to prove, with characteristic recourse to practical experiment, that Gothic architecture too must be the outcome of realising in stone the essential characteristics of an earlier wattle construction. He presented this theory to the Royal Society of Edinburgh in 1797 and published his ideas in the same year as his *Essay on Origins and Principles of Gothic Architecture* with a new edition in 1813, the year the house was completed. Sir James went so far as to construct a miniature cathedral, based on the 'Cloister of Westminster Abbey', with 'poles of ash three inches in diameter' into which a tracery of wattle was woven with 'willow rods one inch in diameter'. The resulting structure must have been enchanting and, since the summit of its thatched roof was eight feet high, it could even be walked through. Sir James asked the artist Alexander Carse to supply a perspective view to provide the frontispiece of the book, and the original drawings for the plates are now in the collection of the Royal Institute of British Architects. Unfortunately the engraved version of Carse's drawing misses out his preliminary study of a seated rustic craftsman weaving the intricate construction like a spider creating its web. Hussey reported a surely fanciful family legend: 'Eventually the cathedral took root, and some fine willows by the lake are said to owe their origin to the diminutive aisles.'

In 1918, a few years before Hussey's visit, the Halls had sold the estate to Mr Frank J. Usher. The new owner took on 'much of the original furniture and fittings' and employed Mr E. Auldjo Jamieson, of the Edinburgh architects Messrs Sydney Mitchell and Wilson, to modernise the house. It was through

Jamieson that Hussey was able to see the original building accounts. Hussey included a miniature plan of this complex, but surprisingly compact, house that derived from Jamieson's 1920 designs for alterations; pen on linen versions of these are now in the National Monuments Record of Scotland.

Jamieson's modernisation of Dunglass in 1920 was thorough. In the absence of earlier plans, it is difficult to be certain of how much he was asked to change. In several respects his approach was surprisingly conservative for the period; he retained not only the marbling of the entrance but also the 'splendid original Oriental wall-papers of emerald green, on which branches issues from pink or mauve pots'. This proved 'hazardous, as the floors and the ceilings had to be renewed, entailing the use of heavy joists, the insertion of which was difficult without damaging the paper'.

The dining room, by contrast, was transformed with Georgian Revival panelling in dark wood; Hussey felt that 'in a house so unique as this it is a little disappointing to find a return to the conventional Georgian dining-room'. But 'a more sprightly form of décor; for example, a room in the style of Thomas Hope, or in Wyatt's later vein as displayed at Doddington, or by the more restrained apartments of the Pavilion at Brighton', simply did not form part of the repertory of historic styles mastered by Edinburgh's craftsmen and in this thinking Hussey was rather ahead of Scottish taste. The marbling of the central top-lit staircase was covered up with tasteful plaster panels in place of its original painted decoration, which matched the marbled vestibule, sadly not photographed by *Country Life*. The only vestige of Gothic that came through these alterations was in the newly formed boudoir with 'an interesting ceiling, the angles filled by brackets of Gothic fan vaulting, of which the ribs are carried down the wall angle as a reed moulding', but without breaking into a plaster imitation of wattle. Handsome new furniture was commissioned from Whytock and Reid of Edinburgh, examples of which were separately photographed by *Country Life,* but this conformed to Jamieson's Georgian mode through veering to the Chippendale style and the

original Brighton Pavilion-papered drawing rooms were, perhaps inevitably, taken back in time to an earlier Chinese Chippendale feel.

It seems remarkable today that a house that was so carefully restored in 1920 could have become a

liability by the end of the war. The complexity of the Picturesque roofs must have required meticulous maintenance, which cannot have been a priority when the house was requisitioned for use as a school; the plans in the NMRS are marked up with class-rooms and boys' dormitories. The *Inventory of Gardens and Designed Landscapes* by Land Use Consultants mentions a fire in 1947. Charles Brand of Dundee stripped out the salvageable materials but the house survived as a ruin for several years before it was

blown up in 1958 and a new smaller house was
built on the site. Colin McWilliam recorded what
remained in 1954 for the SNBR, taking a fine composite photograph showing the relationship between
the house, the chapel and the stable buildings, but it
did not seem to have made a particularly Romantic
ruin. Hussey featured Dunglass in his own study of
The Picturesque in 1927, illustrating it with a *Country
Life* photograph of the Belvedere tower looking
upwards from the falling ground, with Nasmyth's
balustraded terraces anchoring the house to the landscape setting. It has thus gained a firm place in British
architectural history.

CHAPTER SIXTEEN

Murthly

Perthshire

EXPLOSIVE END FOR A PERTHSHIRE MASTERPIECE

If Murthly is the best-recorded act of demolition in the files of the National Monuments Record of Scotland, it was surely the least typical of country houses. Built in 1831 by James Gillespie Graham for Sir John Drummond Steuart, it was never inhabited, and came to be seen as a folly, the Steuarts' entry in a pointless 'Palace Race' amongst the greater Perthshire landowners. The Marquess of Breadalbane won with Taymouth, graced in 1842 by the Highland fairytale of Queen Victoria's visit, but it was to prove a hollow victory; as a result of their sheer extravagance, the once-proud Breadalbanes had to sell off their vast house to a hotel company in 1920. Murthly itself was abandoned as an empty shell in 1832, though the Steuarts could console themselves with the thought that they had got rather further than the Duke of Atholl's Gothic Palace at nearby Dunkeld, designed by Thomas Hopper in 1828, which had not even been roofed by the time of the Duke's death in 1830; the family subsequently retrenched to homely old-fashioned Blair.

This first photographic study of Murthly is taken from the archives of *Country Life*, but when Lawrence Weaver called, in 1915, it was to record the old-fashioned Scotch Baronial topiary garden and the ancient tower house, where the family resided. He knew the architect and date of the 'New' House at Murthly, a mere few hundred yards away, but saw it as an aberration, an empty unfinished shell whose only salient point was that it 'forms a spectacular background to the formal garden':

> The building is as melancholy an example as one could hope to meet of a great enterprise begun and never consummated. It stands as a grim reminder of human unwisdom and serves no better purpose than a back-cloth to the theatre of the garden.

The next thirty years saw little change in this attitude, and when demolition was proposed there was no lamenting. Indeed, it was presented as an act of progress, as reported in the *Evening Telegraph* on 8 October 1948: 'The New Castle, Murthly is to be demolished to make "ballast" for the Hydro Electricity Board's power dam at Pitlochry.'

Country Life's view of Murthly in 1915 also shows the handsome avenues of trees that are such a feature of the estate, and a tennis court erected in front of the unfinished mansion

OPPOSITE: This detail of the entrance front shows the unfinished stone stairs and a makeshift timber stair erected by the demolition agents

It was a decision characteristic of the period, presented by the newspaper as its owner's patriotic duty:

Mr D. Stewart Fotheringham, the present laird, is unmoved by the removal of the present house. He says it has never been of any use, except when it was used as an Ammunition Store during the last war. Once or twice a dance was held in the ballroom.

'It would have been demolished long ago,' he said, 'but the task of pulling it down was not considered a commercial proposition. But when materials are so badly needed the enormous tonnage will make a valuable contribution to building projects.'

Given the Laird's dismissive view of this portion of his inheritance, it is hardly surprising that the newspapers made light of New Murthly's historical interest, one commenting cheerfully: 'When the castle is blown up bang will go a link with the days when Perthshire lairds vied with each other in building white elephants.' Murthly's nineteenth-century assets, locked up in a whimsically aristocratic and inflated mansion, were now seen as being released to serve more worthy modern and democratic purposes.

It was perhaps these unusual circumstances and the lack of any sense of a heritage that mattered a straw, so different from the sad levelling of historic Panmure, that led the Dundee demolition contractor, Charles Brand, to view this job as a highlight in a long career of destruction. He was at pains to photograph his firm's on-site skills in action and, since newspaper publicity was important to his firm's continuing prosperity, to ensure there was press coverage at every stage. No other house is so well covered in his files of press cuttings and the record in his photographic albums, neatly wrapped in brown paper for their better preservation like school textbooks, goes so far as to be entitled 'Demolition Step by Step', an exemplar in case another Murthly needed to be disposed of.

Charles Brand asked his photographer to include portraits of all the principals engaged in the demolition, including the Laird, the explosive experts and his own staff as well as Mr A.H. Young of the Hydro-Electric Board and Mr J.E. Henderson, their architect. Brand's enthusiasm for recording his projects was normally confined to a single photograph which was converted in a pencil drawing by an artist, Colin Gibson, to join a collection confusingly called 'etchings'; one would like to think of these, suitably framed, hanging like big-game trophies in the firm's business premises at 45 Commercial Street, Dundee.

The photographs and newspaper accounts build up into a 'how to do it' demolition manual. Brand's foreman, James Wilson, told reporters from the *People's Journal*: 'We are taking the roof off first. . . Most of it will be useless, although the heavier timbers, mostly of pitch pine, is grand stuff. The joists have been hand-dressed from the finest material of that time.'

Wilson was resourceful and had 'brought off a novel idea . . . dislodging the 4 corner towers by jerking them off their foundation by a cable attached to a tractor'. He had 'walked across 6 inch planks 144 feet up when dealing with the massive central tower' but his 'worst moment' came on these skied planks when a 'squadron of bats swept out of the tower' and nearly toppled him off. His men then 'sawed through the rafters 50 feet up'. Brand's photographic survey includes a view of this extracted timber neatly stacked up below the lofty turrets, and the wood was declared 'as good as when erected'.

The walls then came down in a series of controlled explosions. The photographs include a photo-opportunity shot of Mr David Faulds, an explosives expert from Imperial Chemical Industries, 'who brought down the massive structures of the Crystal Palace and who can make masonry of any height fall just the way he wants it'. In preparation for these explosions, 'two Glasgow men, Walter Brash and James Brown, have been boring the 3 feet thick walls with powder charges'. There were 700 bore holes packed with explosives two feet from the ground and Mr Brash commented that 'the blast will lift the whole building at once, before it collapses and comes crashing down . . . it will be a sight worth seeing'.

The blasting proceeded in what Brand's men

The entrance front 'less Towers' with the cupolas pulled off and the extracted timber neatly stacked for reuse elsewhere

called 'nibbles', biting off individual chunks of the Castle, a sequence confirmed in the photographs, until only the central tower was left standing. The final blast was treated as a county social event, as the *Evening Telegraph* reported on 26 January 1949 under the headline 'BIG BANG AT MURTHLY': 'The Laird and his sister and hundreds of people assembled to witness the spectacular blast' but sadly the 'sightseers' had to contend with 'a drizzle of rain'. Mr Faulds faced an additional test because the Laird's modern garage was a mere twelve feet from the blast zone; he had buffered it under timber for safety. At '3.20 crouched behind a tree, Mr Faulds pressed the button connected to the fuse'; there was 'an ear-splitting roar, and the masonry blew up in a thick cloud of dust'. 'Rubble piled up against the timbers' cocooning the garage, but thankfully 'it was unharmed'.

These successive blasting operations produced '36,000 cubic yards of first-class stones' of which the best went to build thirty-five new houses at Pitlochry and a further twenty-nine at Tarbert, designed by the architect J.E. Henderson for the Hydro-Electric Board's workmen. The stone was also used to repair the parapet of Dunkeld Bridge.

Worthy as all this redistribution was at the time, over half a century later there must be a real fear that a masterpiece had been destroyed unwittingly. New Murthly's patron, Sir James Archibald Steuart, was an amateur of architecture and the house presumably encapsulated his ideas. Born in 1794, he succeeded his father as the Sixth Baronet in 1827, and embarked on his immense project shortly afterwards, as a bachelor in his early thirties. The building of New Murthly looks much more like a young man's

ABOVE: 'Mr Faulds, ICI Explosive Expert, Wiring up
Explosives'

RIGHT: Brand's photograph shows their precision blasting
taking down the castle in manageable stages

BELOW: Mr Young, of the Hydro-Electric Board, measuring a
large stone after the first blast

BELOW RIGHT: '*Left to right*, Mr Brand, Mr Boyd, Estate
Factor, Mr D. Steuart Fotheringham, Laird of Murthly, Mr
A.H. Young, Hydro-Electric Board, and Mr J.E. Henderson,
Architect – Surveying Blasting'

'Blasting of East Corner'

exercise in architectural connoisseurship than the antler-locked dynastic competition with his neighbours that legend asserts. Sir James's handsome draughting-table still survives, an appropriately antiquarian piece, in Dutch marquetry. Of even greater moment is the collection of architectural drawings, mostly theatrical in subject, that his widow bequeathed to the newly founded Royal Institute of British Architects following his death. With sheets by Boullée, Juvarra, Oppenord, Hubert Robert and Vanvitelli, they formed a worthy foundation for this great national cabinet of architectural drawings, now

housed in the Victoria and Albert Museum. They have proved a more enduring monument to Sir James than the New Murthly; when they were exhibited in May 1981 the accompanying pamphlet stated: 'many of the drawings in the collection, although described as stage designs, are simply displays of virtuosity in draughtsmanship, and this clearly was the aspect that attracted Sir James for he seems to have possessed an unerring eye for quality . . .' Two theatrical paintings from his collection are now in English Heritage's collection at Marble Hill House.

The designs for Steuart's dream palace at Murthly had many contemporary admirers. Sir Walter Scott confided to his journal on 3 July 1830 that he 'went to look at the drawings for repairing Murthley, the house of Sir John or Sir James Stewart now building by Gillespie Graham, in which he has planned after the fashion of James VI th's – a kind of bastard Grecian – very fanciable and pretty though'. The Earl of Ashburton deemed the drawings to be 'perfectly beautiful'.

Steuart's choice of the Jacobean style, with 'buckle-quoins' copied from George Heriot's Hospital, must have alluded to the ancient lineage of the Stewarts, who had been settled at nearby Grantully for centuries and who only acquired Murthly in 1615. The building history is well documented in payments to tradesmen, including John Steele who supplied the heraldic carvings, a tribute to the quality of the execution, but most exciting of all for modern art history are the sums paid to the young Augustus W.N. Pugin for 'models'.

In her *Pugin*, published in 1975, Phoebe Stanton quotes from a fragment of autobiography where Pugin claimed:

> at this time I designed all the interior
> decoration of a large Mansion for Mr Gillespie
> Graham. They included a great Hall, chapel,
> entrance hall and staircase, ante-room, Library
> and Drawing room all with the exception of the
> last in the style of James 1 st. The drawing room
> in the style of Louis 14th.

The long and extraordinary relationship between Gillespie Graham and the much younger Pugin has been explored by James Macaulay in *Architectural History*, Volume 27. In the romantic version of the story, Pugin was shipwrecked on the Firth of Forth and, after being rescued, applied to Gillespie Graham for aid. As Dr Macaulay shows, Pugin also recorded that he was introduced to Gillespie Graham in September 1829 – when Pugin was a mere seventeen years old. Although much remains unclear, the design of Murthly had a central role in the start of this relationship. In spite of Pugin's youth he had, allegedly, been designing furniture for Windsor Castle since 1827 – although Sir Hugh Roberts has tempered this by suggesting in *For the King's Pleasure* (2001) that the boy was more probably assisting his father A.C. Pugin in the detailing of these designs. The collaboration begun at Murthly was to develop in unexpected ways and Pugin also appears in the Murthly accounts as supplying 'carvings' for £105; Dr Macaulay records that he had made survey sketches of English prodigy houses including Audley End and Hatfield to assist in the design of the New Murthly, 'the first important Jacobean mansion in nineteenth-century Scotland'.

The question of what exact role Pugin and Gillespie Graham played is not easy to unravel, and it becomes even more difficult if we try to seek the patron's part in this gourmet Jacobean pie. No other Scottish architect at this period had Gillespie Graham's theatrical flair for designing interiors. However, if we look at the pen presentation plan in the Collection of the Royal Incorporation of Architects in Scotland, it is difficult not to see in its swirling excesses of circulation space the untempered hand of the amateur. The enormously deep plan has a broad transverse corridor whose central compartment was labelled 'The Great Tower' and this space, at the heart of the House, soars up into the ogival dome over the largest central tower, making one think of Fonthill. This transverse corridor led to the grandest of Imperial staircases on the right-hand side of the plan, and this was extravagantly supported by a number of back stairs. On the main axis, the broadest flight of external steps, rivalling Hopetoun – and never actually built – led up a further broad internal flight under the Tower to a long Great Hall

LEFT TO RIGHT:

'The Final Blasting'

'View of Rubble after Large
Stones have been selected'

'East View – after Blasting'

serving as the dining room, placed like a Palladian saloon, to resolve, in true Hollywood style, into the biggest of canted Jacobean bays. To the right of the Hall was a domestic chapel. On the left-hand side of the plan was a long suite of reception rooms with a central octagonal drawing room dividing another long drawing room from the parlour and library. On the right of the plan, the Great Stair divided two bedroom suites with the private rooms at the front of the house and a state bedroom, an unusual specification in the late 1820s, to the rear. This spreading plan, with its corner turrets, has an inflated scale, but it is clear that this was a thoroughly modern late Georgian Country House, rather than any Jacobean pastiche, and its spaciousness made it easy to eat up and digest Pugin's Louis XIV drawing room too.

There is a sense that much of the pleasure in all this must have lain in the actual design process and the parcelling up of all this extravagant space into the plans that were so much admired by architectural connoisseurs; surely the design would have been tempered by the harsh realities of a Perthshire winter, with only the experimental heating systems then on offer. Another version of the plan, pasted in the album of the Glasgow architect Charles Wilson and now deposited in Strathclyde Regional Archives, has a more gallery-like transverse corridor paced out with columns. Although they are neither pasted in contiguously with the plan, nor entirely congruous with it, the Charles Wilson album also includes a number of watercolour presentation perspectives of the new rooms. One, with skied suits of armour and a Hatfield staircase just glimpsed off stage right, has the feel of a young person's work and it is tempting to attribute it to Pugin. Gillespie Graham took up this kind of perspective with gusto and it is possible that his relationship with Pugin inspired his use of this kind of drawing, while Pugin's skills must have been developed by his own experience of assisting with the sumptuous fully furnished perspectives produced for the ageing George IV at Windsor, to show how the fruits of the king's lifetime of collecting would look in their intended places at the Castle.

But these interiors were destined to remain a dream sequence. The New Murthly was roofed in 1831, and one of the last entries in the accounts is from the painter, Buchan, who in 1832 gilded the phalanx of weathervanes made by Robert Riches that

spun on their pinnacles over each of the many turrets. Then the work was abruptly stopped, seemingly on Sir James's marriage in 1832 to Jane, daughter of the Earl of Moray, and the house remained an empty shell awaiting its nemesis at the hands of Messrs Brand of Dundee and ICI's explosive expertise.

In 1837 Sir John took the surname of Drummond-Steuart after succeeding to his mother's estates at Logiealmond, and he died without a son in Paris in May 1838. His brothers also pursued unusual and exotic paths. His next brother and heir William, born in 1795, had gone to America where he became fascinated with Red Indian culture and converted to Catholicism, while their younger brother Thomas, known as the Abbé Steuart, withdrew to the monastery of Monreale near Palermo in Sicily. When William returned home, accompanied by a native companion and servant, Antoine Clement, he introduced a herd of buffalo to Murthly. Although William is supposed to have fallen out with Sir John over the patrimony that was frittered away by New Murthly, the architectural drawings, now in the Collection of the Royal Incorporation of Architects in Scotland, tell a different story. Gillespie Graham had initially been employed at Murthly to make additions to the old Castle by Sir John's father in 1822 and the presentation portfolio includes sections of a saloon and new Regency library. But astonishingly, far from abandoning it after Sir John changed his mind, Gillespie Graham drew up an even more megalomaniacally extravagant proposal for New Murthly in 1840, comprising an immense 300-foot Jacobean 'conservatory', situated at right angles to the principal façade, with a glazed arcade towards the flower garden, in whose capacious sub-basement were a long chain of domestic offices and a kitchen connecting by a staircase in a link-building to the piano nobile of the New Castle.

Sir William made no attempt to realise these ideas; instead his interest focused on the ancient chapel in the grounds at Murthly, which was rebuilt by Gillespie Graham to create a family mausoleum as well as the most sumptuous Roman Catholic private chapel in Scotland, with Byzantine Revival icons by Alexander Christie. This patronage was celebrated in a fittingly resplendent cutting-edge chromo-lithographically printed monograph – a triumph of Edinburgh book production in 1850.

Murthly had one last surprise as a 'Lost House'. In July 1980 Marcus Binney and John Harris of Save

Magnus Jackson's photograph shows the panelling of Pugin's Louis XIV drawing room as erected in the Old Castle

Britain's Heritage published *Lost Houses of Scotland*, in preparation for which they went through the photographic file for each house in the National Monuments Record of Scotland and visited the sites. Attracted by Murthly, they published the interior photograph of the drawing room from the collection of glass-plate negatives by the Perth photographer Magnus Jackson, who had made a complete survey of the art collection at Scone for Lord Mansfield. His glass plates had been printed up by the National Monuments Record of Scotland which, unaware of the twists and turns of the estate's history, assumed they were from New Murthly. When this view was published, they were put right by the then Laird, who pointed out, to their embarrassment, that the room was still very much intact in the Old Castle. Obviously at some point, possibly following a fire

in 1845, the surviving interiors intended for New Murthly had been transferred to the Old Castle. The Magnus Jackson plates also include this view of the dining room with its hammerbeam ceiling and it seems probable that the dining room, in the form of a Great Hall, and Pugin's Louis XIV drawing room, were also originally intended for New Murthly. There is still much of this rich and complex story to disentangle.

Tourists attracted to Perthshire today may enjoy watching the iridescent salmon bravely tackling the salmon leap during their visit to the Pitlochry Dam, but it is interesting to speculate if they might not have enjoyed a visit to the shell of the largest unfinished house in Scotland even more. New Murthly's epitaph was written in 1937 by Sir John Stirling Maxwell, a founder of the National Trust for

Scotland, who had been inspired to publish his *Shrines and Homes of Scotland* by his daughter, who had asked him to recommend a book on the historic architecture of Scotland, and ended up writing it for her himself:

> Among nineteenth-century architects Gillespie Graham (1777?–1855) has had less honour than he deserves. It is said that A.W. Pugin, whom he befriended when shipwrecked in the Forth, helped him with the design of the spire of the Assembly Hall which is such an outstanding feature of Castle Hill . . . The design of the new castle at MURTHLY in Perthshire was certainly his own. Based on Jacobean models, this unfinished house, for dignity, proportion and beauty stood quite alone in its day and is still without a rival.

Magnus Jackson's photograph of the dining room in the Old Castle shows the hammerbeam ceiling intended for the Great Hall of the New Castle

CHAPTER SEVENTEEN

Abercairney and Millearne

Perthshire

SPECIAL PLEADING FAILS TO SAVE TWO PERTHSHIRE GOTHIC MANSIONS

Country Life's articles on two demolished houses in Perthshire, Abercairney and Millearne, written by Mark Girouard in 1961 and Alistair Rowan in 1972 respectively, reflect the revolution that was occurring in the perception of this type of early-nineteenth-century Picturesque Gothic house. Neither article was campaigning in tone. It was accepted that the 'cost of maintaining and running' Abercairney was an unreasonable burden while Millearne 'though striking and attractive to visit' could 'never have been easy to run'. Yet the mere fact that two serious architectural historians were turning their attention to such deeply unfashionable houses and attempting to teazle out their history and the architects responsible, accompanying their text with superb photographs, was a powerful piece of advocacy on their behalf. This focus of attention was the more remarkable in the context of *Country Life*'s attitude to the Scottish country house since its foundation in 1897.

The magazine had traditionally turned to Scotland much as it turned to the chateaux of France, in a holiday mood to enliven its weekly diet of English country-house fare. Visual qualities were primary and the magazine sought out the conventionally photogenic ancient Scottish tower houses like Glamis, Craigievar and Traquair. It was a boon for Scotland when Lawrence Weaver was appointed as architectural editor in 1910 because he got on well with Sir Robert Lorimer, Scotland's leading architect, whose own new work was imbued with the visual character and charm of Old Scots architecture and thus well suited to the needs of the magazine. Weaver's unique achievement was to wean the readership away from tower houses with pioneering articles on the early Scottish classical houses of Sir William Bruce and James Smith.

But the magazine was simply not interested in nineteenth-century architecture of either the Scotch Baronial or the Picturesque Gothic kind. As late as 1954, when its publishing arm, Country Life Limited, published John Fleming's

FAR LEFT: The bay window of Abercairney's drawing room looking west, 'full of light and glitter' with its white and gold paper and green damask pelmets

LEFT: The theatrically 'narrow and confined' Gallery at Millearne was furnished in antiquarian style under fanciful pierced Gothic arches

The east entrance front of Abercairney with the tower, added in 1869

Scottish Country Houses and Gardens Open to the Public, drawing on fifty years' worth of accumulated glass plate negatives, photographs of Abbotsford, the cradle of the Scotch Baronial, had to be borrowed in from elsewhere. These articles on Abercairney and Millearne were thus a highly unusual departure from the magazine's usual Scottish coverage and it was no less unusual to include demolished houses in the weekly Country House series.

Mark Girouard's two Abercairney articles are impressive in valiantly attempting to put into context a then very unfamiliar cast of Scottish architects. The patrons at Abercairney were Colonel Charles Moray, who began the new house in 1804, leaving it an unfinished shell on his death in 1810, and his son, James Moray, who completed it during the 1840s;

the tower was added by the architect R. Thornton Shiells, a Gothic specialist, in 1869. The Morays were one of the longest-established families in Perthshire and Abercairney was well documented. When Charles Moray embarked upon a new house to replace its eighteenth-century predecessor in 1803 he consulted two London-based architects, Archibald Elliot and Charles Heathcote Tatham, but it was built to the designs of Richard Crichton, 'an Edinburgh man'. Following his death in 1817, it fell to his nephews and successors Richard and Robert Dickson to complete the house.

Girouard attempted to place the family's decision to build a new-fangled Gothic Abbey in a wider social and historical context, as befitted the writer who would go on to publish the definitive

history of the *Victorian Country House* in 1971. In 1961, however, the architectural genre still required some special pleading: 'There is as a whole something a little absurd about early Gothic-Revival houses: they can be odd and amusing and enjoyable to visit, but it is hard to take them altogether seriously.'

A particular strength of Abercairney was that so much of its original decorative finishes were still intact, and Girouard had thus to explain to his readers that much of what appeared to be solid oak was merely plaster vaulting grained to imitate more costly carpentry. The mastery of these new-found skills of graining and marbling by contemporary firms of house painters was part of a revolution in taste at this time. A portion of this graining at

Abercairney was carried out by the young David Roberts, who was on the way to establishing himself as an independent artist, via a spell as a painter of theatrical scenery; the company of actors who employed him had failed and he was obliged to return to house painting. He thus, he recalled, 'entered into an engagement with Mr Irvine in Perth as foreman and principal workman . . . I was chiefly employed at Abercairney, a very large mansion newly erected'.

Abercairney had also retained many of its original wallpapers, which were no less rare than Roberts' graining. With the exception of the single stool shown in the photograph, the suite of gilt Empire seat furniture made for Cardinal Fesch, Napoleon's step-uncle, had already been sold, along with the

The east compartment of the Abercairney library with McInnes's portrait of Colonel James Moray in full Highland dress and double doors leading along the enfilade to the drawing rooms

The big drawing room at Abercairney at the west end of the enfilade, with gold and white paper and green damask curtains

carpet, shortly after the war, but Girouard wrote inspiringly about this room's ability to stimulate and give visual pleasure in the face of the house's relentless decline:

> The big drawing-room at Abercairney, however, was in a class of its own: its proportions, its colour and its decoration fused together to make a room that was a real delight to be in. By great good fortune it retained its original wallpaper, colouring and curtains . . . The paper was white and gold; the curtains were of green damask . . . The room was a very light one; and the criss-cross of the vault combined with the diapered wallpaper to enclose it in a kind of network of white and gold.

It was demolished soon afterwards and its owners, like those of Millearne, moved to a smaller, more practical house on the estate.

Millearne was a much less ambitious house, with a stronger thread of architectural amateurism, but it spoke strongly to the young Alistair Rowan, who described his article as an 'illustrated obituary':

> It was a wonderful place. Gawky and awkward and never long concealing the piece-meal process by which it came into being, it had a charm that is often denied to more organised architecture. Its development is an intriguing puzzle, and as an example of a moment in the history of architectural taste it was a building of rare value.

By 1972, when Millearne met its fate, a skeletal framework of Historic Buildings Grants was in place in Scotland and the government officials responsible were making serious efforts to understand the history of the unfashionable Gothic Revival houses that seemed to be particularly strongly threatened by demolition. But the owners of Millearne did not want to pursue this course and Rowan was given permission to publish his two articles on Millearne only after the house had been demolished. When Jonathan M. Gibson arrived to take his photographs, the foundations of the new house were already under construction and impeded his attempt to provide a visual elegy to match Rowan's text.

Rowan played a leading role in the Historic Buildings Council for Scotland's reassessment of these houses. His doctoral thesis had been devoted to Robert Adam's Castle Style and Early Gothic Revival houses in Scotland, which led him to explore the influence of this aspect of Adam's oeuvre on the next generation of architects. During these researches he worked on the architectural history of Taymouth Castle in Perthshire, the greatest of all the leading Gothic Revival houses in Perthshire and one that has miraculously survived. He published his exciting new discoveries about the architects and craftsmen responsible for this masterpiece in *Country Life* in 1964 and later joined the staff of the magazine; after his appointment as a lecturer in the Fine Art Department of Edinburgh University he began to contribute articles on other Scottish houses.

The main thrust of Rowan's doctoral thesis was incorporated by Iain MacIvor in *Castellated and Gothic Houses in Scotland 1745–1840: A Report to the Historic Buildings Council* (1964). As Professor David Walker recalls, the taste of officialdom at this time, like that of *Country Life*, then stopped short with some firmness at the Georgian, and the sudden appearance of a highly articulate and charming young academic, well able to argue the merits of these despised and threatened buildings, reversed the balance in their favour. Rowan also credited the help given to him by

ABOVE: General view of the east corridor at Abercairney

ABOVE LEFT: Detail of the vaulted ceiling of the east corridor at Abercairney, described by Mark Girouard as 'an elaborate and highly successful Gothic fantasy with extraordinary hanging arches of wood separating the different portions of the arched vault'

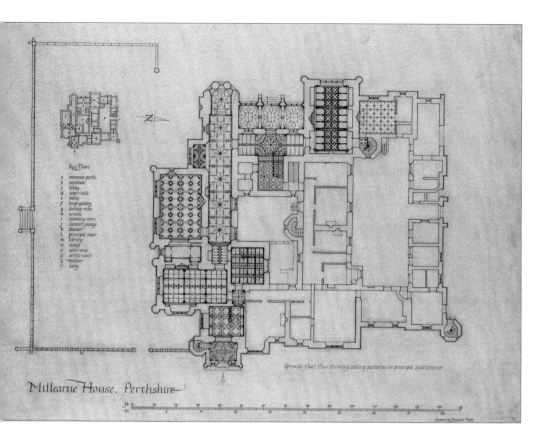

Ground-floor Plan showing ceiling patterns in principal apartments

Millearne House. Perthshire

Dr James Macaulay, whose own study of this genre, published as *The Gothic Revival* (1975), also signifies the profound change in attitudes that had occurred at this time.

Millearne was built by a younger son, John George Home Drummond, on a moderate estate and was thus very different from Abercairney, the seat of a leading country family. The second son of Sir George Home Drummond of Blair Drummond, Home Drummond had been left an independent fortune and purchased Millearne estate, with its existing contemporary house, in 1821. The Home Drummonds were related through marriage to the Morays of Abercairney and Alistair Rowan surmised that R. and R. Dickson may have helped in the building of the new 'irregular Gothic' house; John George Home Drummond himself certainly took a leading role in the design of the building, which was erected in a piecemeal fashion between 1823 and 1838, with the dates of each portion often carved into the stonework with his initials. The result was anything but coherent, but, as Rowan explained, 'irregularity' was a primary aesthetic aim of some of the most advanced architecture at this time: 'historically, Home Drummond and R and R Dickson did a

RIGHT: The dining-room
ceiling at Millearne, copied
from the plate of the roof
of Crosby Hall in London,
published in Pugin's
*Specimens of Gothic
Architecture* (1821)

remarkable job, for when Millearne was finished it
had a plan more rambling and irregular than almost
any other house of the date'.

Rowan went on to describe the varying volumes
of the individual rooms, whose heights rose and
fell just as the differently sized windows produced
passages of light and darkness as one toured the
house. Jonathan Gibson's photograph of the roof-
scape vividly shows the rambling effect – 'and in the
end it required two public and three service stairs
to make it work'. It was perhaps a measure of its
sophistication that much of the detailing was copied
from Augustus Pugin's *Specimens of Gothic Architecture*
(1821). Unfortunately, for readers of *Country Life*, 'In
its latter days [the library] was used as a storeroom
and cannot be illustrated, though its high blue painted

ceiling with decorated cusps taken from Pugin, its
solid oak book cases and immense stone fireplace
combined to create a memorable interior.'

Both these articles on Abercairney and Millearne
were thus describing houses already in decline.
Alistair Rowan with great fairness showed that
almost from the outset it had been a difficult house
to run and quoted an 1867 letter from Agatha Home
Drummond, the sister of its patron and writing
after his death: 'This beautiful house has been a great
trouble and anxiety to me, from the difficulty there
has been to get it properly kept. It is quite a grief to
me to see what my dear John was so fond of either
neglected or ill used.'

The *Country Life* photographic record of Abercairney had been supplemented with photographs taken

in 1956 by Colin McWilliam, with a further record set by David Walker. Characteristically, the former captured the last valiant attempts to make an attractive home in an unfashionable house, with bowls of hyacinths and comfy-looking sofas in the Small Drawing Room and a vase of daffodils on the table in the small dining room in preparation for lunch, with the kind of classic late Georgian furniture that contemporary taste preferred to the Gothic or Antiquarian.

Millearne was even more fortunate – in a mark of the new appreciation of these Gothic Revival Houses, a very detailed record – including the ceiling, fireplace and mezzanine galleries of the partly dismantled but very ambitious library – was made for the nation prior to the demolition by Geoffrey Hay of the National Monuments Record of Scotland, the first time the Record had made such a comprehensive record of so relatively modern a structure. Millearne's complex design can now be fully studied and appreciated through the long written report or 'Record Sheet', with its superb measured drawings, including one showing the varying ceiling patterns, and the many photographs of the individually carved chimneys and the other quirky details, which still have the power to engage new admirers.

CHAPTER EIGHTEEN

Fintray

Aberdeenshire

MODERNISED SEAT OF THE SEMPILL FAMILY, SACRIFICED TO SAVE ANCIENT CRAIGIEVAR

Superficially, Fintray might be just another statistic: a relatively modest Aberdeenshire granite country house that saw a spurt of mushroom growth in the Tudorbethan style in around 1830 at the hands of John Smith of Aberdeen, who built Balmoral for Queen Victoria. It was requisitioned in 1940 at the start of the Second World War and restored to its owners, Lord and Lady Sempill, in 1946. But the Sempills also owned Craigievar Castle, and could not afford to keep both going after the war. The choice between Craigievar, one of Scotland's best-loved buildings, and the deeply unfashionable Fintray was not a hard one and the latter was demolished, unmourned, in 1953. And yet, as a sacrificial house, Fintray played a crucial role in the preservation of Craigievar Castle, and thus surely deserves an honoured place in the national architectural consciousness. In comparison with photogenic Craigievar, the record of Fintray is slight and the article about its demolition published in *The Scotsman* on 20 February 1953 has the only known view of its impressive central saloon.

Both the Craigievar and Fintray estates had been held by the Forbes family since 1610. William Forbes had altered the existing tower house of the Mortimer family at Craigievar into the celebrated architectural masterpiece that miraculously survives today by 1625–6, the dates on its innovative new moulded plaster ceilings, while Fintray, although much closer to Aberdeen on the banks of the Don, remained a secondary seat architecturally, the date of its building unknown. But perhaps because of a certain remoteness, Craigievar seems to have stopped evolving somewhere around 1740, when the modern buffet niche was inserted into the Great Hall. Fintray began to nudge ahead, certainly by the late eighteenth century, when the surveyor Peter May made a surely rather fanciful survey plan of the estate for Sir Arthur Forbes (1709–73), with corkscrew groves of trees. Alongside the rather ramshackle open courtyards of the Old House is a block fronting the Pleasure Gardens marked as the New House. By 1793, when Sir William Forbes and his wife, Sarah, began to improve Fintray to equip it as the family's ordinary residence, it had totally outstripped Craigievar, which was no longer inhabited.

LEFT: Pre-war photograph of the dining room at Fintray. The austerity of Burn's interiors is relieved by the phalanxes of gilt-framed family photographs of the Forbeses of Craigievar, with the Raeburn portraits of Sir William and Sarah Forbes on the left and right of the fireplace

This careful stewardship was soon imperilled by the workings of a disastrous trust intended to provide for the younger children in the early nineteenth century, and the next laird, Sir Arthur, was so irresponsibly profligate that he died a bankrupt in Calais in 1823. His steadier younger brother, Sir John Forbes of Craigievar, a judge in the East Indian Service, had to come home and pick up the pieces of a seriously embarrassed estate. In 1824 his architect, John Smith of Aberdeen, delivered his now celebrated report on Craigievar as 'well worth being preserved as it is one of the finest specimens of the age and stile in which it was built, and finely situated'. As a result Craigievar was to remain carefully preserved, used only as an informal holiday for late-summer shooting parties, where 'roughing it' in the old-fashioned castle was part of the fun.

With Craigievar decreed unalterable, Sir John decided to enlarge and modernise Fintray, and inevitably he turned again to Smith. Smith produced a rather sprawling courtyard plan, incorporating much of the existing house, but with the modish distinction of a circular courtyard, presumably copied from James Playfair's Cairness, the most innovative house in Aberdeenshire. Smith's plans for

this house survive at Craigievar and there is a specification for the circular court in the family muniments along with his estimate of January 1827 that 'a new mansion house of Granite stone in the Grecian Style' incorporating part of the present house would cost £6,000. But then, suddenly, the documents reveal a new sense of ambition as Sir John decided to approach William Burn, Scotland's leading country-house architect. The boldness of this decision, when money was tight, is perhaps reflected in the unusual completeness of the documentation for Fintray, which must have been a very minor commission for Burn while being Sir John's major architectural undertaking. For his part Burn was at pains to explain his methods and charges with precision to prevent any misunderstandings, while Sir John made careful drafts of his letters to Burn. In his draft of his initial letter of approach, Sir John explained that he was proposing to build a new house and name-dropped that he had taken the advice of Lord Blantyre and Mr Wallace of Kelly, near Greenock, suggesting that 'something of the old manor house style will suit my place'.

In his letter of advice to Sir John, Mr Wallace detailed his own improvements at Kelly and the sizes

This unusual wide-angle view of Fintray shows the relation of the entrance front to the terraced side flank, where the public rooms enjoyed views of the River Don

of its rooms and the handsomeness of his sideboard recess as models to be copied but he also advised that 'with Mr Burn I would be very frank', clearly a reference to the available budget. The best way to contain costs was to recast at least part of the existing house. Burn recommended keeping the library and his meticulous grasp of house planning, which was to allow him to move his office to London later as the leading designer of country houses in Britain, is demonstrated in the complex catechism that he despatched to Lord and Lady Forbes as to how various component zones of their household should interrelate alongside simpler questions like what height would they like the public rooms to be. Burn also commended Sir John's proposal to visit Blairquhan in Ayrshire from Kelly, one of his early architectural masterpieces. By April 1828 Burn was finalising the minutiae of the planning with such conveniences as a muniment room off Sir John's sitting room, and was confident and experienced enough in his dealings with his patrons to dismiss Lady Forbes's pet notions.

In March 1829 Burn charged Sir John £100 7s 6d for his finished plans and specifications of the proposed alterations and additions to Fintray. But at some point before September 1828, when Burn responded, Sir John had drafted the rather startling proposal that Smith might be retained to realise Burn's designs, although it would be perfectly understood 'the designs are yours and built by Mr Smith'. It was surely, he continued breezily, 'no uncommon thing for the plans to come from one architect and the work to be executed by another', when he must have known this was an extraordinary suggestion. But Burn took this unusual proposition in his stride and replied saying he had 'no objections to the arrangements you propose and am perfectly satisfied with the employment of Mr Smith' who had been 'most liberal and conciliating with his conduct towards myself', but recommended the employment of an independent clerk of works.

Fintray, as built by Smith to Burn's design, had the stamp of Aberdeen rather than Edinburgh tradesmen. The masons were Duncan Neilson and Hutcheon and their contract was complete by 1832; the carpenter was James Byres, with Dallas and Leith carrying out the plasterwork. But there was nothing provincial about the end result and Burn's surviving working drawings in the family papers reveal its polish and flair, the more especially if it was at least partially cobbled from an existing house, although there is no earlier work indicated on the plans apart from some irregularities of fenestration in the back wall to the office court. Burn devised an L-shaped house with a *porte cochère* leading to an octagonal hall lit by canted windows and then axially, and quite unexpectedly, through to a double-height and top-lit saloon in the angle of the L-shaped blocks, within which a magnificent staircase ascended to the upper floor; this large volume of circulation space at least recalls Blairquhan. To the right of the saloon lay the interconnecting drawing room and library with views to the River Don, with Sir John and Lady Forbes's private suite in line beyond these, enjoying the same views, and with the nurseries conveniently to hand behind. To the left of the octagonal hall and saloon lay the dining room with Sir John's private room and then the kitchens and offices continuing the axis of this block.

Although the antiquarian style chosen for the new building seems to be a fairly serious attempt at Jacobean to harmonise with Craigievar and the date of the creation of the baronetcy in 1630, the interior was classical, perhaps in deference to the vestiges of the previous house, although Burn was no slave to Picturesque notions that there should be a unifying stylistic integrity across a house. The few surviving interior photographs, the splendid saloon excepted, show an austerity of ornament perhaps bordering on astringency, and the house-painter's bill by Henderson and Gillespie of August 1837 captures something of its Late Georgian character with its 'common wainscot' in imitation panelling, the staircase 'balusters bronzed', while the '12 busts' they cleaned and painted were probably intended for the '12 brackets' painted earlier by James Gordon in the 'lobby', probably meaning the octagonal hall. The only gilding was limited to the picture rails in the dining room and drawing rooms. The photograph of the dining room may show one of the two marble chimney-pieces supplied by A. Macdonald for £45 and although there was a clearly new suite of Grecian furniture the austerity is only relieved by the phalanxes of gilt-framed family portraits, including Raeburn's portraits of Sir John's parents, among the artist's earliest documented works in 1788.

The documentation also makes clear how it was possible for Sir John to contemplate the building of Fintray at a time when the estates were in real financial difficulties. In his account book he quotes the legislation that facilitated this and countless similar building projects throughout the land: 'An act to encourage the improvement of Lands, Tenements and hereditement in that part of Great Britain called Scotland held under Settlement of Strict entail.' This law enabled owners of entailed estates to offset the cost of such improvement down through the next generations and made less likely the kind of crisis that had faced Craigievar, when the need to provide for Sir John's six sisters had forced the sale of unentailed portions of the estate. The papers show that Sir John and his legal advisers meticulously followed the necessary process, beginning with obtaining the consent of his immediate heir.

Requisitioning during the Second World War was the beginning of the end for Fintray and the Dowager Lady Sempill (the Sempill title had entered the family in 1884) moved to a smaller house on the estate, Little Fintray, in 1940. The text of *The Scotsman*'s 1953 article, headed 'unwanted aberdeenshire mansion's demolition', makes clear that Fintray was being sacrificed to save Craigievar, which had remained uninhabited, used only for shooting parties. Regret is tempered by resignation, although the article is deferential to the 'well-known Forbes-Sempill family' and identifies Smith as the 'City Architect of Aberdeen'. In this tax-burdened age, the paper continued: 'Lovers of tradition and architectural beauty have become used to the melancholy spectacle of the show pieces of the country side being torn apart by demolition squads.' The published photographs of the 'stately' interiors may have been taken before the war and were jarringly juxtaposed with an up-to-date photograph showing the roof removed because the 'new owner' had already stripped out the panelling and fittings, leaving only the presumably unsaleable 'shell'. Now an 'even more ruthless death sentence' was proposed as Fintray 'may be blown up'. This was clearly a novel and thus newsworthy concept at the time, not to mention an exercise that would give the detachment

of Royal Engineers in Aberdeen 'useful practice in the art of warfare'. A scheme to turn the house into a children's home failed through the dangerous proximity of the River Don. *The Scotsman* interviewed 'an old farm worker' for his opinion; he responded, 'For a' that's left the quicker the job is done the better, for we dinna like to see the hoose the wye it is noo.'

Very little trace of Fintray survives today at Craigievar as Lord and Lady Sempill had to make some hard decisions about what could be salvaged. Although most of the earlier, and thus smaller, family portraits were taken, even the relatively modest scale of the two Raeburn portraits seemed daunting in comparison with the diminutive spaces at Craigievar and they could only be hung together over the fireplace in the Queen's Room. A pair of smart rosewood card-tables listed at Fintray in 1816 had to be separated at Craigievar and take on a new role as dressing tables. But almost everything else had

to be sold and, while Fintray may be forgotten, some of these former possessions have acquired a posthumous glamour. The large painting shown hanging on the saloon staircase in the *Scotsman* article is now in the National Gallery in London, having been purchased by the perspicacious Sir Denis Mahon in 1954, and is now recognised as *Cumaean Sybil with a Putto*, one of 'Guercino's finest late works'. A photograph of one of the smaller sitting rooms at Fintray, although difficult to identify from Burn's plans, shows part of the collection of Meissen porcelain which has an impeccable provenance; surviving bills prove it was purchased directly at the factory by Sir Arthur Mitchell (1708–71), Ambassador to the Court of Frederick the Great and a native of Aberdeenshire, who was to leave much of his estate to his friend the Laird of Craigievar. Happily, a few of the surviving plates were recently purchased for display in the buffet niche at Craigievar by The National Trust for Scotland.

View of a sitting room at Fintray with a copy of the celebrated 'Craigievar' card-table on the left of the fireplace and part of the collection of Meissen porcelain inherited through Sir Arthur Mitchell

CHAPTER NINETEEN

Guisachan House

Inverness-shire

ADAM REVIVAL DECORATION IN THE HEART OF THE HIGHLANDS

During the second half of the nineteenth century, improvements in railways, roads and steamers meant that the unspoilt scenery of even the most remote Scottish Highlands became easily accessible for those with the wealth and leisure to take full advantage of its charms. A prime example of how an estate or shooting lodge could be transformed into something dazzlingly exotic was Guisachan in Glen Affrick, which had been owned for centuries by the Frasers of Culbogie before Dudley Coutts Marjoribanks of the banking family, later to be created Lord Tweedmouth, rented the estate in 1854 and purchased it in 1856.

Tweedmouth had many ideas for his new property, and the resources to carry them out. He kept the outside of the house conventional enough in an austere classical style, although he greatly enlarged it with bay windows, an elaborate conservatory and cast-iron crestings crowning its mansard roofs. But the interior was to blossom into the earliest cycle of Adam Revival decoration in Britain. Lord Tweedmouth's championship of Georgian decorative arts had its origins in his initial enthusiasm for English eighteenth-century porcelain, with an early specialisation in blue Wedgwood jasperware. With few rivals in this field, Tweedmouth amassed an outstanding collection of Wedgwood, including original designs commissioned by Josiah Wedgwood from Flaxman, which he kept at Guisachan, whose public rooms were redecorated to harmonise with the collection and show it to advantage.

Tweedmouth's daughter Ishbel, in her *Reminiscences*, describes how 'every year after our arrival home my sister and I were allowed to help my mother in taking all the treasures from their cupboards, washing them, and putting them in their places'. Wedgwood plaques were incorporated into both the chimneypiece and the walls of the drawing room, whose focus was one of the finest of the Wedgwood vases, standing on a commode between a pair of windows and reflected in a large pier-glass. This may have been the vase, designed by Flaxman and with a relief depicting *The Apotheosis of Homer*, whose pair was purchased by Lord Tweedmouth in 1877 for £735. The rest of the room was panelled in

LEFT: The drawing room at Guisachan, photographed by Lady Aberdeen with her mother, Lady Tweedmouth, reading on the sofa to the right. The room was decorated in the Adam Revival style to complement Lord Tweedmouth's outstanding collection of Wedgwood jasperware

Exterior view of the east front of Guisachan, screened by an ancient tree with the extensive conservatories leading to the dining-room pavilion

Aesthetic style with inset decorative paintings under a ceiling in the Adam style that successfully unified this unusually thoroughly worked-out interior. A staircase in the upper conservatory led down, under a mural depicting the surrounding scenery with its Scots pines embodying remnants of the ancient Caledonian Forest, to the combined, and impressively large, dining and billiard room, which occupied its own ground-floor pavilion unrestrained by the original compact house plan.

The excellence of this Adam Revival decoration was the result of its having been entrusted to the London firm of Wright and Mansfield, whose expertise must have been developed largely as a result of Lord Tweedmouth's discerning patronage; his daughter recorded that their 'taste and knowledge of the Adam period of decoration was unrivalled'. Wright and Mansfield also decorated Brook House in London for Lord Tweedmouth. Sadly, these

pioneering interiors were to be relatively short-lived; after Lord Tweedmouth's death in 1894 his son sold off first the Wedgwood and finally the estate itself, in 1908. There is no mention of the Adam Revival character of the interiors in the sale catalogue of 1919, when the widow of its new purchaser, the Earl of Portsmouth, put the estate on the market once again. In 1939 the house was purchased by Lady Islington and the interiors were stripped out and their components sold off. The resplendent contemporary interiors at Brook House had been demolished a few years before in 1933 but happily a photographic record was recently discovered in the archives of *Country Life* and shows that its glittering cosmopolitan interiors veered more towards the Louis XVI style than the purer Adam idiom that the Wedgwood collection inspired at Guisachan.

If Guisachan has gone, it has certainly not been forgotten and its fame, for a lost Scottish country

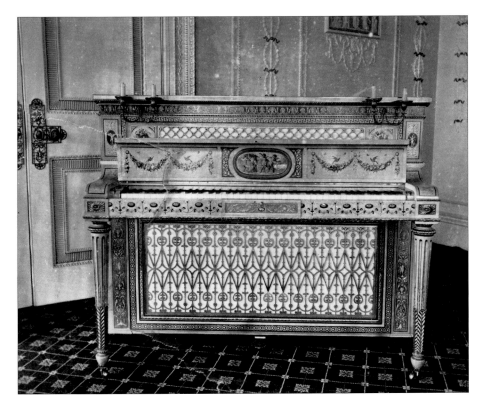

house, is rising. The Wedgwood collection was purchased *en bloc* by Lord Leverhulme, a collector of jasperware and as enthusiastic an admirer of the decorative arts of Georgian England as Lord Tweedmouth, and it remains intact as one of the glories of the Lady Lever Art Gallery in Port Sunlight, keeping memories of Guisachan alive at the Gallery and through its catalogues and publications. When Lord Tweedmouth's daughter Ishbel married the Earl of Aberdeen in 1877, it was perhaps inevitable that his ancestral seat at Haddo House in Aberdeenshire should be thoroughly refitted by her father's pet decorators, Wright and Mansfield. Many of their successful Adam Revival ideas, originally worked out for Guisachan, were copied at Haddo, which has two Wedgwood chimney-pieces and several Wedgwood vase lamps on Adamesque gilt torchères, composition ceilings incorporating decorative paintings and an impressive yardage of the identical crimson and pale-blue trellis carpet seen in the photograph of the Guisachan drawing room. Although the Aberdeens considered Wright and Mansfield's charges to be 'scandalously high' they were consoled by the knowledge that their work was of such quality that it came up as good as new when it was 'thoroughly cleansed over, before our

eldest son came of age'. The Aberdeens' supervising architects at Haddo were Wardrop and Reid of Edinburgh, whose exactly contemporary alterations at Culzean Castle for the Marquess of Ailsa were the first Adam Revival interiors in Scotland to be carried out in a genuine Robert Adam country house. The decorator at Culzean, responsible for the painting and upholstery, was Thomas Bonnar, of Edinburgh, who became a leading figure in the Adam Revival in Scotland. Although the Adam Revival was to become an international style and particularly popular in America, in Scotland the style took on a national character because Robert Adam was recognised as the nation's most celebrated architect.

Haddo has had a happier fate than Guisachan. In 1978 it came into the care of the National Trust for Scotland and its interiors are now the most important cycle of interior decoration in the Trust's care and survive complete with their original furniture, still bearing the labels specifying the room at Haddo that each piece was destined for. The library at Haddo, with its pair of sumptuous Wedgwood chimney-pieces in green jasperware, is particularly well preserved and retains both its original chenille carpet and its couture-cut crimson velvet curtains. Among the many volumes on its olivewood and

ebony bookshelves are the bound albums of photo-graphs taken by Ishbel, an enthusiastic and pioneering photographer, which include these images of her family home. This explains their unusual intimacy, with Lady Tweedmouth herself comfortably ensconced on the drawing-room sofa. The complete-ness of the Haddo interiors has inspired a study of Wright and Mansfield by Dr Eileen Harris in *Furniture History* vol. 32 (1966), which has revealed that their thoroughness was the result of the marriage of their talents: Alfred Wright had been

trained as a cabinet-maker and upholsterer while George Mansfield's family were builders and decorators. Dr Harris has also revealed that the Guisachan piano has found its way to British Columbia.

Guisachan has the unusual distinction among lost houses of Scotland of having its own posthumous guidebook; in 1990 Duncan Fraser published his *History of Guisachan* to answer the many questions that visitors attracted by the scenery posed about the demolished mansion.

View from the south of Guisachan as a ruin, May 1986

LEFT: The upper conservatory led down under a mural of the Caledonian Forest to the combined dining and billiard room on the ground floor

CHAPTER TWENTY

Carbet Castle

Dundee

RICHLY DECORATED JUTE PALACE
OF THE GRIMOND FAMILY

The homes of Scotland's great nineteenth-century industrialists deserve a book to themselves, especially since the evaporation of heavy industry that sustained them means that they figure extensively in the ranks of lost houses. Coltness House, in Lanarkshire, was already an established country house when it was acquired by the Houldsworths, proprietors of the Coltness Iron Works. The authors of *Glasgow and Lanarkshire Illustrated* (1904) described it as 'one of the largest houses in Lanarkshire' – a high claim since these included Hamilton Palace (see Chapter 3). By the time of its final photographs in the NMRS of 1982 it had become a Dr Barnardo's Home absorbed into Motherwell, with little trace left of its carpet-bedded terraces and conservatories.

Ferguslie Park in Paisley was the home of the Coates family, famous for their cotton thread, but by the time of its final record photographs in 1979 it had found a new purpose as the Glencoats Hospital, with twisted iron beds abandoned incongruously below the elegant historicist French Rococo with frivolous scroll-work framing gods and goddesses. Coltness was indistinguishable from other country houses except in its outsize dimensions, whereas Ferguslie was more typical of the type, resembling as it did an inflated villa. A common factor in all these early industrialists' houses was their proximity to the owners' mills and factories, but as communications improved in the late nineteenth century a Glasgow merchant could commute by rail from any number of convenient fantasy locations and sleep at the seaside as easily as up a mountain.

The best known of all these industrialists' homes, and something of a music-hall turn in Scottish architectural history, are the Dundee jute palaces, which anticipated the competitive edge and sheer showing off, on absurdly restricted sites, that has made the 'cottages' of Newport, Rhode Island world famous for architectural excess. These houses are celebrated in their own publication, *Nineteenth Century Mansions in the Dundee Area* (1958), by a young Dundonian, David Walker, now one of Scotland's most distinguished architectural historians. By then the bubble that gave rise to them had long since burst and their deeply unfashionable High Victorian suburban architecture made them a liability for their wealthy owners, who had moved out to country houses in rural Angus or across

LEFT: The dining room at Carbet Castle in November 1984, with its painted ceiling by Charles Frechou still miraculously intact

The Lodge Queen St Church Carbet Cas./Herschel/Dunalister/Loftus/One Ash/S. Margarets/Castleroy/The Hollies/Craig-gowan

E.A

P.47.80 AERIAL VIEW OF BROUGHTY FERRY.

Bird's-eye view of the jute palaces in Broughty Ferry, marked up by Colin McWilliam; many were later demolished

the Tay Bridge into Fife; like the Sharps, for whom in 1906 Lorimer rebuilt Hill of Tarvit, near Cupar, which survives with all its original contents in the care of The National Trust for Scotland.

Born and based in Dundee, and a student at Dundee College of Art, the young David Walker was recruited to the cause of recording the city's vanishing architecture by Colin McWilliam, the Director of the Scottish National Buildings Record, in 1953. Buildings were disappearing fast and it is rewarding to watch Walker's photographic powers improve in the files of the NMRS, although his natural *métier* remained that of a draughtsman and lithography, drawn directly onto the plates, was the chosen medium for his record of the jute palaces.

The accompanying letterpress is both a history of these fast-disappearing mansions and a prose poem to their unique oddities; the text opens with 'Aye it's no' bad. But it's sma' be oors', the apocryphal response of a mill owner being shown over a rival's new house.

Cholera and other health scares and the attractions of the seaside lay behind many industrialists' move to Broughty Ferry, conveniently linked by railway to the Juteopolis, and Colin McWilliam marked up an early Valentine photograph to show their individual villas in their leafy suburb. Although Dundee was not without models for large houses, with nearby Panmure (see Chapter 5) and Burn's noble Camperdown of 1821, the jute barons did

not attempt to rival the noble sobriety of these aristocratic models but preferred more compact villas on their smaller suburban plots, with their distinction lying in their 'rich lush decorations' within.

A new standard was set by Castleroy, whose patron, George Gilroy, asked the Perth architect Andrew Heiton to design a Gothic palace to surpass all others. Built in 1867 on the highest ground in Broughty Ferry, with, in David Walker's words, a 'central hall like a set out of a grand opera', it is visible on the far right of Valentine's photograph.

This inspired Joseph Grimond, owner of Bow-bridge Works in Dundee, to instruct his architect Thomas Saunders Robertson to respond in kind. The

Grimonds' modest villa Kerbat House, which they had bought in 1861, was thus transmogrified on the west side in 1866, with the tower and eastern wings added in 1868 to create the outrageously improbable Carbet Castle. This enjoyed a prominent site in Camphill Road and its threatening silhouette lorded it over the modest fishing port below, its high ivy-clad terraces an extraordinary contrast in scale with the diminutive three-bay Georgian house with its weekly wash hanging out across the road.

The kindest explanation of Carbet Castle's final appearance is that the Grimonds wished to enjoy the view south across the Firth of Tay from all their extensive apartments. But, with rising ground immediately behind, there was nowhere else for the

Camperdown, with its many bay and bow windows facing the Firth of Tay, and dwarfing an earlier more modest villa below

Detail of the carved camel, the Grimond's Factory trademark, on the Gate Lodge, 1984

RIGHT: Detail of the surprisingly small main staircase with its niche on the landing, 1953

house to develop and Walker's few photographs of the back quarters show a lingering Kerbat scale: the

whole front was only a gigantic piece of stage scenery, and the back of the house, jammed against the rising ground, must have been quite an anticlimax.

In his initial extension to the west of the old Kerbat House in 1866, the design for which is more modestly titled 'Carbet House', Robertson added a new Corinthian front door, whose broken pediment framed Grimond's monogram. To the left of this new entrance was the great double bay window lighting the dining room on its ground floor, with the drawing room above. Amazingly this section of the Castle lingered on till 1984, long after the rest had gone to make way for more modestly scaled houses, when I had the good fortune to visit it when it was being recorded by the Investigator, Miles Horsey, and the photographers of the Royal Commission on the Ancient and Historical Monuments of Scotland. By then the exterior had a forbidding aspect; the stumps of the amputated wings had been weather-proofed with more grey cement, the windows were mainly

boarded up and there was decay on all sides. Reduced to a more modest footprint, it had something of the feel, if not the scale, of a standard Scottish suburban house of the period with its double bay for the stacked dining room and drawing room. The staircase had by then fallen in, making the drawing room unattainable, but the dining room, in contrast to the sorry exterior, was still a breathtaking vision of the Paris of Louis Napoleon and the Empress Eugénie. The ceiling, painted and signed by Charles Frechou and dated 1871, with its cheery paired boy and girl cherubs disporting themselves languidly on a diapered ground to suggest the Seasons, had miraculously survived, with enough of

Detail of the drawing-room ceiling in 1953, with a male putto playing the bagpipes and a female putto singing along

the once-lavish gilding still clinging on to reflect the light flooding through the long plate-glass sashes in the two bay windows.

By great good fortune, the even richer decoration of the drawing room, on the first floor and also in the style of Louis XIV, had also been recorded, although in black and white, in 1953 and 1955 when it was still intact. The dining room had a rather Marotesque cornice of paired gilded brackets, whereas the acanthus cornice of the drawing room was ablaze with gilding and had a ceiling of richly framed panels with gilded centre roses and delicately coloured grotesque scrollwork, with rather more animated boy and girl putti playing musical instruments on brilliant blue and pink reserves. The best photographs are the black and white studies by Bernard Wopinski, D.A., which captured the skittish putto playing the bagpipes in a conceit that must have delighted Grimond's guests, as well as the exquisite Pompeian or rather Louis XVI doorcase, with its Wedgwood jasper plaque and dark ground panels recalling ancient frescoes, including a stylish beehive as abuzz with bees as the Grimonds' Bowbridge works with their thousands of workmen. The draw-

ing room's effect must have been intensified by the relatively modest scale of the rather cramped staircase that led up to it, which may have been a survivor from the original house.

David Walker recalled his first experience of this interior some years later:

> for Carbet, my camera was totally inadequate! I originally heard about it from William and Norah Montgomerie; at that time the place was owned by a contractor, so I got the key to the gate and walked in through a broken window, and was absolutely amazed by what I saw!

In his 2001 biography of Joseph's grandson Jo Grimond, the Liberal politician and later Secretary of The National Trust for Scotland, who was born in 1913, Michael McManus says that Carbet was then lived in by an unmarried aunt. But Jo's father lost control over the firm when the family was bought out by the Jute Industries. Carbet Castle was valued at £7,500 and sold off. Castleroy was sold in 1954 to Charles Brand, the Dundee demolition contractor, and recorded in spooky, echoingly empty photographs by the same team who recorded Carbet.

Detail of the richly decorated drawing-room door with its Wedgwood or Sèvres plaque

David Walker had the good fortune to be given access to Carbet's sale catalogue by an uncle who worked in the Jute Industries. Sadly it seems not to have survived and we must be content with his vivid abstract:

> Here we may read of the two organs, the vast furniture, the elaborate mantel suites, the tazzi, the painted spittoons, the statue by Miroy of Paris 'fitted for gas' and the innumerable French clocks 'so that when Twelve o'clock struck pandemonium broke out'.

Walker's summing up of the jute palaces is surprisingly modest:

> The lush decoration has for the most part disappeared either with the houses themselves, or in making them more palateable to recent tastes, and what remains is not, on the whole, of much merit; but at least some of it has an agreeable period nostalgia, still preserving

something of the atmosphere of that vanished luxurious gas-lit world.

But Carbet Castle is surely as fine as anything at Newport. Frechou's decorative painting is of superb quality and it is tantalising to speculate how these rooms were conceived and how much of the work was carried out in Paris; surely the whole conception was that of a French decorator or even an architect. The architect Robertson, according to David Walker, described Joseph Grimond as 'a man of fine taste', who later acquired Peddie and Kinnear's Kinnettles House for his country house, and Michael McManus describes the conviviality of Carbet and Grimond's interest in Robert Burns and his many benefactions. Dundee could ill afford to lose even two fragmentary interiors of such scintillating international quality and it is some slight compensation to know that the dining-room ceiling, at least, was rescued in 1984 and awaits a suitable setting in which its languid cherubs can continue to enchant us.

CHAPTER TWENTY-ONE

Crathes

Aberdeenshire

FIRE IMPERILS A
MUCH-LOVED TOURIST ATTRACTION

Fire continues to present a grievous threat to every country house; a moment's inattention and centuries of history can be wiped out in a flash. The fire at Crathes on 6 January 1966 was particularly shocking because only a decade earlier the Laird, Major-General Sir James Burnett of Leys, had handed over his ancient family seat to the care of The National Trust for Scotland to ensure its preservation for all time. The Burnetts had held Crathes since the time of Robert the Bruce and the Castle's greatest treasure was the venerable 'Horn of Leys', said to be the Laird's badge of office as the resident Royal Forester, which hung proudly over the fireplace in the Great Hall. Crathes was one of the most important of the castles of Aberdeenshire, whose lairds vied with each other over their relative ancientness, and during the nineteenth century it became a popular tourist attraction through its convenient location at Banchory on Royal Deeside, near Aberdeen.

This ancient character was considerably played up after 1876 by its 11th Laird, Sir Robert Burnett, when he returned home after a spell as a sheep farmer in California with his New York wife, Matilda. With an American thoroughness that was unusual in Scotland, they excised more recent attempts at modernisation in a feeble Gothick style to create an Aesthetic vision of period rooms in a more rigorous sixteenth-century mode. The glory of Crathes had always lain in its old oak woodwork, both in the ceiling of the late sixteenth-century gallery (then known as the chapel) at the top of the tower, and the outstanding collection of early oak furniture including a famous bedstead and armchairs. To harmonise with these exceptionally rare survivals, the Great Hall was transformed in 1877 with oak panelling and gilded leather hangings, and the collection was augmented with newly purchased antiques from the same historical period including majolica and a gilded Venetian chair.

Sir Robert's achievements were celebrated by Lawrence Weaver in a 1913 *Country Life* article which featured a thrilling discovery made a few years earlier, when the Georgian lath and plasterwork, now deemed anachronistic, was ripped out to expose complete cycles of Renaissance decorative painting still clinging to the ancient ceiling beams. These fragile and precious decorations, contemporary

LEFT: A dramatic view of the old tower at Crathes by *Country Life* in 1937, using the ancient yews to screen the more modern wing

with the tower itself, were carefully restored and, with the same thoroughness that prevailed throughout the Castle at this time, were complemented by pioneering modern paintings in the same style. These rediscovered ceilings challenged existing perceptions of Scotland's decorative history and greatly increased the antiquarian importance of the Castle. Weaver's photographer was clearly instructed to train his lens upwards on these ceilings because of the density of furnishings below, although for the photograph of the Gallery these have been dramatically thinned out, with no fewer than two leopard skins and one lion's pelt left to demonstrate its length.

When the *Country Life* photographer returned in 1937, there was no longer any need to focus solely on the ceilings because the rooms had recently been beautified with consummate taste by Sir James Burnett and his wife, Sybil, into something that was perhaps now as much a visual showplace as a family home, set in the perfected gardens that were her 'consuming passion'. Oliver Hill deemed Crathes to have 'the most enchanting garden in Scotland' when *Country Life* published his *Scottish Castles of the Sixteenth and Seventeenth Centuries* in 1953. Pleated linen hangings in these painted chambers covered up much of the more recent experimental painted decoration, while the historically dubious late Victorian decor in the Great Hall was stripped back to the ancient rubble wall-faces. The astringency of the effect of going 'back to bedrock' was softened with an equally authentic Italian carved stone chimneypiece and a Knole sofa.

Country Life responded to this photogenic reinvention of Crathes by devoting no less than four articles to the property, with two on the Castle by Christopher Hussey and another on the surrounding gardens by G.C. Taylor, while their resident expert on the decorative arts, Margaret Jourdain, wrote up the exceptionally rare early oak furniture. From the articles it is clear that Sir James and Lady Burnett were pioneering the use of early inventories to understand the Castle's history and purchasing related early oak pieces. Hussey also gives precise dates for the phases of the restoration and states that the painted ceilings had been uncovered as early as 1877.

But after the Second World War the costs of maintaining such an outstanding showplace and its extensive walled gardens led Sir James and Lady Burnett to approach The National Trust for Scotland, which had been founded in 1931 and in 1942 set up its own Country House Scheme based on that the National Trust had pioneered in England, with the aim of keeping both the donor families and their historic collections *in situ*. Sir James and Lady Burnett presented Crathes and its historical contents to the Trust in 1952, making it clear that they were fully in sympathy with its aims, but retaining the Horn of Leys and the earlier charters in family possession. Crathes was soon established as a leading tourist attraction on Deeside, a popular holiday resort with the added cachet of proximity to Balmoral.

No cause for the fire is given in the Trust's own archives but they vividly reveal the sheer relief amid the dirt and devastation in the aftermath of the fire that the ancient tower had narrowly escaped, although the painted decoration had been imperilled by the acrid deposit of soot and blistering from the heat. But the other half of the House, including what were known for convenience as the 'Queen Anne' and 'Victorian' wings, was totally gutted. Photographs show how their interiors, with a solitary ruined painting still dramatically clinging to a blackened wall, had been burnt to a crisp and the furnishings reduced to ash, creating an effect more reminiscent of a coal mine than a stately home.

By great good fortune many of the early charters and the Horn of Leys had been placed in showcases in the gallery at the top of the old tower, thus surviving the surrounding conflagration. Although the Castle was insured, the Trust was now faced with some complex problems that were to take several years to resolve. 'Perhaps the Victorian wing will not be missed' was the sentiment of one Trust member who wrote to console the grieving Director. However, even if it could not be deemed an aesthetic asset, it was nevertheless to this wing that the family had retreated when the Castle was opened to the public, and continuing family presence was a central Trust policy. But when Jamie Cecil, the new laird, came of age, not long after the fire, and changed

The charred remains of the corridors in the destroyed wing, open to the skies but with portraits still in place

his name to Burnett, the only accommodation available for him at his ancestral seat was the mere stump of a service zone of the otherwise gutted Victorian wing. Miss Jean Dodds, the Trust's resident representative, had lost all her possessions when her flat was burnt out.

The architect Schomberg Scott, the Trust's 'Adviser on Architecture and Furnishings', was rapidly on the spot to survey the damage and to suggest a way forward. His perceptive initial report, dated 8 January 1966, suggested the course of action

finally adopted by the Trust, though not before it had to weather a mass of well-meaning private and official meddling as the Trust's officials grappled with insurance claims for the gutted wings and missing contents, obtained the necessary planning permissions for both the demolition of the ruins and the rebuilding, and submitted every stage of the decision-making process to its own formidable committees and the relevant external bodies, including the Historic Buildings Council for Scotland and the Royal Fine Art Commission. There was no shortage of advice volunteered to the Trust from all quarters, ranging from purists at one extreme who wanted to see the ancient tower stand alone untrammelled by any subordinate buildings to enthusiasts for modern architecture who saw an opportunity in this disaster for a trailblazing new commission. The architect F.R. Stevenson urged the Trust to have the strength of character for a show of 'modern expressionism', citing Le Corbusier's Ronchamp Chapel as an exemplar; the more conservative Trust officials were aghast at such iconoclasm.

The essence of Schomberg Scott's scheme was that only the Queen Anne wing should be retained, but rebuilt to its original proportions of a mere two stories, and that the Victorian wing should be completely demolished. It was not immediately clear, however, if the surviving walls of these wings would be strong enough to sustain even this modest reconstruction. The raggle of masonry on the newly exposed wall where the Queen Anne wing abutted the ancient tower clearly demonstrated how the roof had been raised at a subsequent period. Schomberg Scott had the good fortune to have the support of the celebrated antiquarian Dr W. Douglas Simpson, Librarian of Aberdeen University and the leading authority on castles in north-east Scotland, who wrote, 'the eighteenth-century wing should be retained. Its Queen Anne dignity gives the exact counter-poise to the élan of the ancient tower and the composition is perfect'. He carried the argument.

The immediate task was to treat the painted ceilings. Since 1961 these had been entrusted to the care of the Stenhouse Conservation Centre, a joint initiative founded by the Trust and the Ancient Monuments Branch of the Ministry of Works. This programme was continuing when the fire broke out and Ian Hodgkinson of the Centre was soon redeployed in removing successfully the damaging sulphurous soot from the ceilings of The Green Lady's and the Nine Nobles' Rooms.

The final insurance claim was settled at £65,000 but this had to cover a number of purposes that were difficult to reconcile, and it was to take over four years to resolve them. Accommodation was immediately needed for the Trust's own representative and the Castle was soon reopened to the public but, mindful of the Burnetts' stress on the 'enjoyment of visitors' at the time of their gift, the Trust particularly wanted to improve the facilities for tourists, whose numbers had been increasing year by year; the limitations of receiving them after the fire within the confined spaces of the surviving tower tended to concentrate attention on the deficiencies. This demand could not but be in conflict with the need to provide the Burnetts with a new home on the site of the Victorian wing, with all the complications of preserving their privacy in a building whose primary purpose was to be accessible to the public. After several plans had been drawn up and subjected to endless discussion, the view of the Historic Buildings Council for Scotland prevailed and it was resolved to devote half the insurance monies to building the Burnetts a self-contained new house nearby, but not visible from the old Castle. Although the Trust commissioned the designs for Sir Jamie Burnett's new home, it was deemed desirable that he should be allowed to choose his own architect, and he decided on the Aberdeen firm of Cowell Mathieson and Partners.

Today, forty years after the fire, the scars have healed and so successful is Schomberg Scott's reconstruction of the Queen Anne wing, whose understated new lower roofline defers politely to the ancient turrets, chimneys and crockets soaring above, that few visitors can have any inkling of the violent recent history. One of the last great Scottish designers of ornament in the tradition of Sir Robert

Lorimer, Schomberg Scott's new reception area for visitors already has a very considerable period charm with its warmth of heraldic colouring and his distinctive wallpapers inspired by further archaeological rediscoveries of early Scottish painted ceilings. In his capacity as the Trust's 'Advisor of Furnishings', as well as its architect, Schomberg Scott rearranged many of the rooms in the old tower to give each a distinctive character, such as his 'Victorian bedroom', that is still visually appealing today, though it reinforces the showplace atmosphere. It is only in

Snapshot of the Victorian
wing by Colin McWilliam in
1956, showing it smothered
by Lady Burnett's creepers

Exhibition drawing by
Schomberg Scott following
the fire, showing his
proposed new truncated
Queen Anne wing

the more recent Family Room on the top floor of the tower, where the genealogical run of family portraits has to be eked out with black and white photographic reproductions from the survey fortuitously undertaken in 1965 by the Scottish National Portrait Gallery, that there is a real sense of loss.

Inevitably there is now a new interest in the Victorian work that was so casually demolished unmourned in 1966. All that survives of it now is a set of extremely handsome wooden doors that may have been in storage in the Court of Offices since Sir James and Lady Burnett's improvements in the 1920s. Their quality makes one regret that nobody had the forethought to make an adequate photograph record of the ruins of the Victorian wing before it

was demolished. The negatives of the 1913 *Country Life* survey have captured an oblique view of this wing but it was inevitably cropped off the published view. The most attractive photograph of the wing is a relatively casual snap of 1956 by Colin McWilliam, which reveals a building of great charm with generous granite bays overlooking the garden and a turret-like garden door, although there is a sense that their almost smothering creepers are an attempt by Lady Burnett to camouflage this unfashionable architecture. Surely today the Trust would have cherished the Victorian additions had they survived, while their voluminous circulation spaces would have added to the pleasures of the visitors' tours.

The NMRS Demolition File

Reproduced here is the NMRS Demolitions File, the only official
attempt to record all Scotland's lost country houses.

Montgomerie House, Ayrshire

Montgomerie House after demolition

Abbotrule House *Roxburghshire* Demolished May
1956

Abercairney Abbey *Perthshire* Demolished 1960

Aden House *Aberdeenshire* Derelict

Airdrie House *Lanarkshire* Demolished c. 1950

Airlie Park *Angus* Demolished

Allanbank House *Berwickshire* Demolished 1969

Allanton House *Lanarkshire* Demolished

Alloa House *Clackmannanshire* Demolished 1955/6

Almondell House *Midlothian* Gutted c. 1950, blown
up 15.6.1969

Altyre *Morayshire* Demolished c. 1962

Alva House *Clackmannanshire* Demolished

Amisfield *East Lothian* Demolished 1928?

Anniston House *Angus* Demolished

Archerfield House *East Lothian* Gutted for grain
drying 1962/3

Ardencaple *Dunbartonshire* Gutted (but for tower)
1957

Ardo House *Perthshire* Demolished

Ardwell *Wigtonshire* 19th C. additions demolished
1956

Aros House, Mull *Argyllshire* Blown up c. 1960

Ashcliff *Angus* Demolished before 1939

Auchaber House *Aberdeenshire* Mostly demolished
1927

Auchindarroch *Argyll* Demolished c. 1969

Auchinvole *Dunbartonshire* Gutted, partially
demolished 1965

Auchry House *Aberdeenshire* Demolished July 1967

Auchterlees *Aberdeenshire* Reduced to single storey

Auchtyfardle House *Lanarkshire* Demolished Feb.
1957

Auldbar *Angus* Demolished Aug. 1964

Aviemore House *Inverness-shire* Demolished c. 1964

Aytonhill *Fife* Burnt and demolished June 1969

Balbardie House *West Lothian* Mainly demolished
1955/6

Balconie House *Ross and Cromarty* Blown up c. 1968

Balgarvie House *Fife* Demolished c. 1938–48

Balgowan *Perthshire* Demolished

Balgreggan *Wigtonshire* Demolished 1966

Balkail House *Wigtonshire* Demolished c. 1960

Ballechin House *Perthshire* Demolished 1963/4

Balmae House *Kircudbrightshire* Blown up 1963/4

Balruddery *Angus* Demolished 1965

Bankton House *East Lothian* Gutted by fire
31.5.1966

Barbarrow *Wigtonshire* Burnt 1942

Barnton House *Edinburgh* Demolished c. 1920

Beechwood *Angus* Demolished

Belfield House *Ayrshire* Demolished 1970

Belton House *East Lothian* Gutted 1956, blown up
12.3.1967

Benholm Castle *Kincardineshire* 19th C. house gutted

Biel *East Lothian* 19th C. additions demolished 1950s

Blackadder *Berwickshire* Demolished

Blackhall Castle *Kincardineshire* Demolished 1946

Blackyell House *Dumfriesshire* Burnt 1929

Blair Drummond *Perthshire* Demolished for new
house

Blythswood House *Renfrewshire* Demolished

Boghead *West Lothian* Demolished c. 1955

Bogie House *Fife* Gutted 1935

Bonhard Castle *West Lothian* Burnt and blown up
April 1962

Bonnington *Lanarkshire* Burnt c. 1900

Boquhan *Stirlingshire* Demolished

Braco Park *Aberdeenshire* Demolished 1968

Brahan Castle *Ross and Cromarty* Demolished to 1st
floor level c. 1953

Brisbane House *Ayrshire* Demolished 1939/40

Broadmeadows *Berwickshire* Demolished c. 1915 for
new house

Broomfield House *Glasgow* Demolished

Broxmouth Park *East Lothian* Early work demolished
c. 1955

Brucklay Castle *Aberdeenshire* Gutted 1953

Buchanan Castle *Stirlingshire* Gutted 1953/4

Burnside House *Aberdeenv* Demolished 1939

Calder Hall *Midlothian* Demolished 1970 after
dereliction

Cambo House *Fife* Burnt 1878

Candacraig *Aberdeenshire* Burnt c. 1900

Cantray House *Inverness-shire* Demolished

Caponflat House *East Lothian* Demolished c. 1947

Carbet Castle *Angus* Demolished before 1939

Cardean House *Perthshire* Demolished 1953

Cardoness *Kircudbrightshire* Mostly demolished
c. 1959

Carmichael House *Lanarkshire* Gutted

Carnock House *Stirlingshire* Demolished c. 1941

Carnousie House *Banffshire* Demolished

Craigend House, Stirlingshire

Faichfield House, Aberdeenshire

Glenormiston House, Peebleshire

Carnousie Old House *Banffshire* Derelict

Carnwath House *Lanarkshire* Demolished 1970

Castlemilk House *Glasgow* Demolished 1965–74

Castle Newe *Aberdeenshire* Demolished post 1950

Castleroy *Angus* Blown up 1953

Castle Wigg House *Wigtonshire* Gutted

Cavers House *Roxburghshire* Gutted 1952/3

Charterhall *Berwickshire* Demolished for new house 1960s

Clermiston House *Edinburgh* Demolished 1970

Coldoch House *Perthshire* Demolished c. 1965

Congalton *East Lothian* Demolished c. 1927

Costerton House *Midlothian* Derelict and roofless

Cowden Castle *Perthshire* Demolished

Cowdenhill House *West Lothian* Demolished c. 1970

Craigbarnet House *Stirlingshire* Demolished c. 1951

Craigend House *Stirlingshire* Victorian section demolished 1968/9

Craighall *Fife* Permission to demolish 1955

Craig House *Aberdeenshire* Burnt 1942

Craigleith Hill House *Edinburgh* Demolished 1955

Craiglockhart House *Edinburgh* Demolished

Cromarty Castle *Ross and Cromarty* Demolished 1772

Crummock House *Ayrshire* Demolished 1968

Culdees Castle *Perthshire* Demolished 1967

Cushnie New House *Aberdeenshire* Demolished 1959

Dales, Peterhead *Aberdeenshire* Gazebos demolished after 1947

Dalserf House *Lanarkshire* Demolished 1963

Delvine House *Perthshire* Demolished

Doonside House *Ayrshire* Demolished 1961

Dormont *Dumfriesshire* Blown up

Douglas Castle *Lanarkshire* Demolished 1937

Dreghorn Castle *Edinburgh* Demolished 1955

Drumfin House *Argyllshire* see under Aros

Druminnor Castle *Aberdeenshire* Additions demolished 1961

Drumdryan House *Edinburgh* Demolished 1958

Dryburgh House *Angus* Demolished

Dryden House *Midlothian* Demolished 19th C.

Dryfeholm House *Dumfriesshire* Demolished

Duloch House *Fife* Demolished 1954/5

Dunbog House *Fife* Gutted

Duncrub *Perthshire* Demolished 1950

Dunglass House *East Lothian* Gutted 1947, demolished 1950s

Dunipace House *Stirlingshire* Demolished

Dunira House *Perthshire* Mostly demolished

Dunnonbie *Dumfriesshire* Demolished 1966/70

Dunottar House *Kincardineshire* Demolished Aug. 1959

Dupplin Castle *Perthshire* Demolished Aug./Oct. 1967

Earlston House *Kircudbrightshire* Demolished c. 1954

Easter Elchies *Morayshire* Additions demolished c. 1950s

Ellishill House *Aberdeenshire* Gutted by fire

Edmonstone House *Midlothian* Demolished

Eglinton House *Ayrshire* Gutted 1930s, blown up

Elderslie House *Renfrewshire* Demolished 1920

Ellon House *Aberdeenshire* Mostly demolished 1920s

Elphinstone Tower *East Lothian* Demolished 1964/5

Faichfield House *Aberdeenshire* Demolished July/Aug. 1969

Farington Hall, Dundee *Angus* Burnt 1913

Ferguslie House *Renfrewshire* Demolished c. 1920

Fernhall, Dundee *Angus* Demolished pre 1939

Fernieside House *Edinburgh* Demolished 1957

Ferntower *Perthshire* Blown up 1963

Fetteresso *Kincardineshire* Demolished 1954

Fetternear House *Aberdeenshire* Burnt 1919, gutted

Fintray House *Aberdeenshire* Demolished 1952

Fordell House *Fife* Demolished January 1963

Forres House *Morayshire* Demolished May/June 1971

Fotheringham House *Angus* Blown up 1963

Frendraught House *Aberdeenshire* Demolished c. 1947

Fullarton House *Ayrshire* Demolished 1967

Garlet House *Clackmannanshire* Demolished Oct. 1964

Garnkirk House *Glasgow* Demolished

Garscadden House *Glasgow* Demolished April 1959

Garscube House *Dunbartonshire* Demolished spring 1955

Gask *Perthshire* Drastically altered

Gelston Castle *Kircudbrightshire* Gutted 1950s

Genoch House *Wigtonshire* Gutted

Gilbertfield Castle *Lanarkshire* Gutted 1950s, demolished

Gilmerton House *Edinburgh* Demolished 1950s

Glasserton House *Wigtonshire* Demolished c. 1954

Glassingal House *Perthshire* Demolished 1966

Glencoe House *Argyllshire* Wings removed 1965

Glenmuick House *Aberdeenshire* Demolished 1948

Glenormiston House *Peebleshire* Demolished 1956

Glenquoich Lodge *Inverness-shire* Demolished 1955

Gordon Castle *Morayshire* Wings demolished c. 1955

Grangepans House *West Lothian* Demolished 1906

Greenlaw House *Midlothian* Demolished 19th C.

Guisachan House *Inverness-shire* Gutted

Halleaths House *Fife* Demolished

Hamilton Hall House *Midlothian* Demolished c. 1830

Hamilton Palace *Lanarkshire* Demolished c. 1929

Hartfield House *Dunbartonshire* Demolished

Hatton House *Midlothian* Fire 1952, demolished 1955

Hawkhead House *Renfrewshire* Demolished

Hazel Hall, Dundee *Angus* Demolished pre 1939

Hazelhead House *Aberdeen* Demolished c. 1956

Heathcot House *Kincardineshire* Demolished

Hedderwick Castle *Angus* Demolished

Hedderwick Hill *East Lothian* Blown up 1961

Helmsdale Castle *Sutherland* Demolished 1970

Herbertshire Castle *Stirlingshire* Burnt c. 1914, demolished

Herdmanston House *East Lothian* Gutted and demolished

Hoddom Castle *Dumfriesshire* Additions demolished 1956

House of Hedderwick *Angus* Derelict

Inchbrakie House *Perthshire* Demolished

Inchdairnie House *Fife* Demolished

Inchrye Abbey *Fife* Demolished from 1960

Inverardoch House *Perthshire* Demolished

Inverclyde House, Hartfield *Dunbartonshire* Gutted 1966

Inverliever Lodge *Argyll* Blown up 1966

Jardine Hall *Dumfriesshire* Demolished June 1964/5

Jerviston House *Lanarkshire* Demolished 1966/7

Johnstone Castle *Renfrewshire* Demolished c. 1950

Kenmure Castle *Kircudbrightshire* Gutted 1950s

Kenmure House *Lanarkshire* Demolished 1950s

Kennet House *Clackmannanshire* Demolished March 1967

Kerse House *Stirlingshire* Demolished c. 1958

Kinbroon House *Aberdeenshire* Demolished c. 1937

Kincraig *Fife* Demolished 1969

Kinkell Castle *Ross and Cromarty* Derelict

Kirkton House *Lanarkshire* Demolished Jan. 1959

Ladykirk House *Berwickshire* Demolished 1967

Langhaugh House *Selkirkshire* Demolished 1960

Langholm Lodge *Dumfriesshire* Demolished 1953

Langton House *Berwickshire* Mainly demolished

Largie Castle *Argyllshire* Demolished 1953

Largo House *Fife* Gutted

Lassendrum *Aberdeenshire* Burnt 1920s

Lauchope *Lanarkshire* Demolished 1963

Laws *Angus* Demolished 1966

Leask *Aberdeenshire* Burnt 1927

Lethamhill House *Glasgow* Demolished 1965–74

Smeaton Hepburn, East Lothian

Linburn House *Midlothian* Demolished 1955
Lindertis House *Angus* Blown up Dec. 1955
Linlathen House *Angus* Mostly demolished
Linthouse *Glasgow* Demolished
Loch Castle *Perthshire* Fire in 1930
Logan Tower *Midlothian* Demolished 1966
Logie House, Dundee *Angus* Demolished 1910
Logie House *Perthshire* Demolished Jan./Mar. 1970
Lyndhurst, Dundee *Angus* Demolished pre 1939
Macbie Hill *Perthshire* Demolished 1950s
Mains House *Dunbartonshire* Demolished
Mains of Badenscoth *Aberdeenshire* Mainly
    demolished 1937
Masterton House *Midlothian* Demolished 1938
Mauchline House *Ayrshire* Demolished 1930s
Mauldslie Castle *Lanarkshire* Demolished 1935
Maulsden House *Angus* Demolished June 1963
Mertoun House *Berwickshire* Additions demolished
    1953
Midhope *West Lothian* Derelict
Millbank House, Arbroath *Angus* Demolished July 1969
Milliken House *Renfrewshire* Demolished *c.* 1935
Milton Lockhart House *Lanarkshire* Demolished
Mollance *Kircudbrightshire* Demolished
Monboddo House *Kincardineshire* Demolished
Moncreiffe House *Perthshire* Burnt *c.* 1958
Montblairy House *Banffshire* Demolished
Montgomerie House *Ayrshire* Burnt, demolished 1969
Mordington House *Berwickshire* Demolished 1973
Mount Alexander *Perthshire* Demolished late
    19th C.
Mount Annan House *Dumfriesshire* Gutted 1930s
Murie *Perthshire* Demolished 1938/9
Murthly Castle *Perthshire* Blown up 1949
New Hall *East Lothian* Demolished *c.* 1909
Newton Hall (new) *East Lothian* Blown up 1966
Newton of Condie *Perthshire* Fire 13.3.1866, ruin
Niddrie Marishal House *Edinburgh* Fire Dec. 1959,
    demolished
Ninewells House *Berwickshire* Demolished 1964
North Barr House *Renfrewshire* Demolished
Old Meldrum Manse *Aberdeenshire* Demolished
    1957/8
Old Neilsland House *Lanarkshire* Demolished May
    1971
Orangefield House *Ayrshire* Demolished Feb. 1966
Ormiston House/Hall *East Lothian* Gutted *c.* 1940
Otterston House *Fife* Demolished *c.* 1950
Panmure House *Angus* Blown up Dec. 1955
Parkhill House *Aberdeenshire* Demolished *c.* 1960

Newton Hall, East Lothian

Parton House *Kircudbrightshire* Demolished Feb. 1964
Peel of Drumry *Glasgow* Demolished 1956
Penicuik, garden villa *Midlothian* Demolished
Petmathen House *Aberdeenshire* Demolished 1955/6
Philiphaugh House *Selkirkshire* Demolished 1965–70
Philorth House *Aberdeenshire* Fire 25.3.1915
Pinacclehill House *Roxburghshire* Demolished 1965–70
Pirn *Peebleshire* Demolished 1950
Pitcorthie House *Fife* Demolished 1950s?
Pitcullo House *Fife* Demolished 1954/5
Pitfour House *Aberdeenshire* Demolished 1927
Pitlurg House *Aberdeenshire* Fire 1927, in ruins
Pittyvaich House *Banffshire* Demolished July 1968
Polkemmet House *West Lothian* Demolished
Polmaise Castle *Stirlingshire* Blown up 1966
Polmont Park House *Stirlingshire* Demolished 1959
Poltalloch House *Argyllshire* Gutted 1957
Raeden House *Aberdeen* Demolished *c.* 1956
Ralston House, Paisley *Renfrewshire* Demolished 1934
Rankeillor House *Fife* Demolished *c.* 1956
Ravenstone Castle *Wigtonshire* Gutted, ruin
Redcastle *Ross and Cromarty* Derelict
Relugas House *Morayshire* Demolished *c.* 1955
Riccarton House *Midlothian* Demolished 1956
Rodney Lodge, Perth *Perthshire* Demolished 1900
Romanno House *Peebleshire* Demolished 1950s
Rosebank House *Dumfriesshire* Demolished
Rosebank, Roslin *Midlothian* Demolished *c.* 1950
Rosehaugh *Ross and Cromarty* Demolished 1959
Rosemount House, Montrose *Angus* Derelict
Roseneath Castle *Dunbartonshire* Blown up 1961
Rosshill (Rossell) House *Ayrshire* Demolished pre 1939
Rossie Castle *Angus* Gutted *c.* 1957
Rossie Priory *Perthshire* Partly demolished *c.*1949
Rothiemay Castle *Banffshire* Derelict
St Fort House *Fife* Demolished 1953
St Mary's Tower, Birnam *Perthshire* Gutted

Smeaton, East Lothian

Sands *Fife* Demolished pre 1950
Sauchie Old House *Clackmannanshire* Partly
    demolished *c.* 1960
Saughton Hall *Edinburgh* Demolished 1954
Saughton House (Old) *Edinburgh* Fire 1920,
    demolished
Schaw Park House *Clackmannanshire* Demolished
    spring 1961
Scotstown *Aberdeenshire* Demolished pre 1947
Seacliff *East Lothian* Fire before 1939
Seaton House *Aberdeenshire* Burnt 1963
Skellatur *Aberdeenshire* Derelict
Smeaton Hepburn *East Lothian* Demolished *c.* 1948
Smeaton *East Lothian* Demolished *c.* 1948/9
Snaigow *Perthshire* Demolished *c.* 1964
Spottiswood House *Berwickshire* Demolished *c.* 1948
Springwood Park *Roxburghshire* Demolished *c.* 1954
Stenhouse *Stirlingshire* Demolished 1960s
Stonebyres *Lanarkshire* Blown up 1939/40
Strichen House *Aberdeenshire* Gutted *c.* 1954
Tarvit House *Fife* Blown up Nov. 1963
Terregles *Dumfriesshire* Blown up 1964
Thirlestane House *Selkirkshire* Blown up Nov. 1965
Thurso Castle *Caithness* Demolished
Thurston *East Lothian* Demolished 1952/3
Tinwald Downs *Dumfriesshire* Demolished 1950s
Tonley House *Aberdeenshire* Demolished
Torbanehill House *West Lothian* Demolished for road
Torry House *Fife* Part demolished
Troup House *Banffshire* Demolished 1960s
Tullibody House *Clackmannanshire* Fire, demolished
    c. 1961
Tullichewan Castle *Dunbartonshire* Blown up 1954
Turnerhill House *Aberdeenshire* Demolished 1930s
Ulva House, Skye *Inverness-shire* Burnt 1954
Ury (Urie) House *Kincardineshire* Demolished 1956
Valleyfield House *Fife* Demolished pre 1939
Wallace's (Benholm's) Tower *Aberdeen* Rebuilt in
    Tillydrone Road
Wallyford *Midlothian* Demolished 1948
Wardhouse *Lanarkshire* Gutted
Warriston House *Edinburgh* Demolished 1965
West Shandon House *Dunbartonshire* Blown up 1965
Williamfield House *Ayrshire* Demolished
Wishaw House *Lanarkshire* Demolished 1953
Woodhall, Port Glasgow *Renfrewshire* Demolished
    pre 1939
Woodhouselee *Midlothian* Demolished 1965
Woodslee, Penicuik *Midlothian* Demolished *c.* 1967
Woolmet *Midlothian* Demolished 1953

SELECT BIBLIOGRAPHY

See also within individual chapters for books relating to a specific house or architect.

Binney, Marcus, Harris, John and Winnington, Emma, *Lost Houses of Scotland*, London: Save Britain's Heritage (1980)
Dean, Marcus and Miers, Mary, *Scotland's Endangered Houses*, London: Save Britain's Heritage (1990)
Gow, Ian, *Scottish Houses and Gardens*, London: Aurum Press (1997)
Strong, Roy, Binney, Marcus and Harris, John, *The Destruction of the Country House, 1875–1975*, London: Thames & Hudson (1974)
Worsley, Giles, *England's Lost Houses*, London: Aurum Press (2002)

PICTURE CREDITS

INDEX

Page numbers in italic refer to illustrations

HAMILTON PALACE

FIRST FLOOR

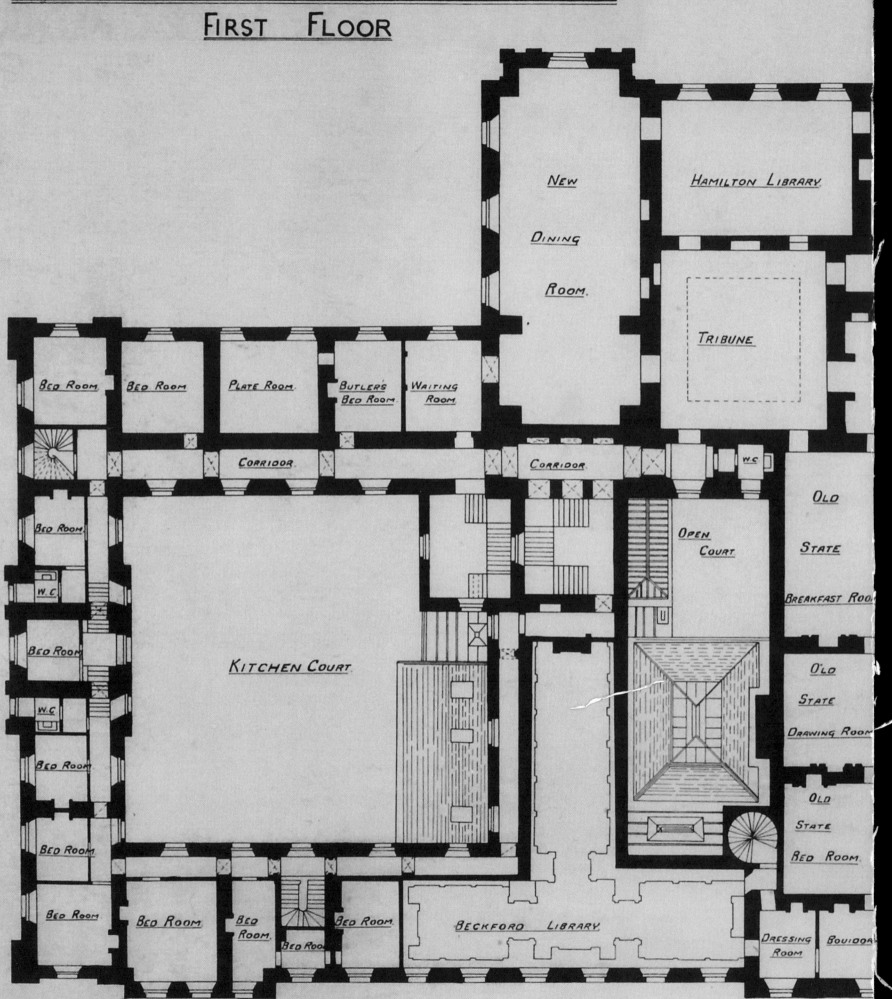

NEW DINING ROOM.

HAMILTON LIBRARY.

TRIBUNE

BED ROOM. | BED ROOM. | PLATE ROOM. | BUTLERS BED ROOM. | WAITING ROOM.

CORRIDOR. | CORRIDOR. | W.C

OLD STATE

BED ROOM.

W.C

BED ROOM

W.C

BED ROOM.

OPEN COURT

BREAKFAST ROOM

KITCHEN COURT.

OLD STATE DRAWING ROOM

OLD STATE BED ROOM.

BED ROOM. | BED ROOM. | BED ROOM. | BED ROOM.

BED ROOM

BECKFORD LIBRARY.

DRESSING ROOM | BOUDOIR